BEST POEMS

Advanced Level

Poems for Young People

with Lessons for Teaching the Basic Elements of Literature

a division of NTC/Contemporary Publishing Group
Lincolnwood, Illinois USA

Cover Design: Steve Straus **Cover Illustration:** Dennis Lyall
Interior Design: Steve Straus **Interior Illustrations:** Pat Doyle

ISBN: 0-89061-893-3 (hardbound)
ISBN: 0-89061-849-6 (softbound)

Published by Jamestown Publishers,
a division of NTC/Contemporary Publishing Group, Inc.
4255 West Touhy Avenue
Lincolnwood (Chicago), Illinois 60646-1975, U.S.A.

8 9 0 QB 0 9 8 7 6 5 4 3 2 1

ACKNOWLEDGMENTS

Acknowledgment is gratefully made to the following publishers, authors, and agents for permission to reprint these works. Every effort has been made to determine copyright owners. In the case of any omissions, the Publisher will be pleased to make suitable acknowledgments in future editions.

Abeel, Samantha. "Self Portrait," reproduced with permission from *Reach for the Moon*, © 1994 by Samantha Abeel and Charles R. Murphy. Pfeifer-Hamilton Publishers, 210 W. Michigan Street, Duluth, MN 55802.

Angelou, Maya. "Caged Bird" from *Shaker, Why Don't You Sing?*. Copyright © 1983 by Maya Angelou. Reprinted by permission of Random House, Inc.

Barrington, Judith. "VI" of the "Villanelles for a Drowned Parent" from *History and Geography*. Published by The Eighth Mountain Press, Portland, Oregon, 1989. © 1989 by Judith Barrington. Reprinted by permission of the author and publisher.

Berry, James. "Girls Can We Educate We Dads?" from *When I Dance*. Copyright © 1991, 1988 by James Berry. Reprinted by permission of Harcourt Brace & Company and The Peters Fraser and Dunlop Group, Limited.

Brooks, Gwendolyn. "truth," © 1991 by Gwendolyn Brooks. Published in *Blacks* by Gwendolyn Brooks, © 1991. Reprinted by permission of the author.

Buckley, M. T. "Birthday" by M. T. Buckley from *Berkshire Review*, Vol. XI, No. 2, Winter 1976.

Cummings, e.e. "old age sticks," copyright © 1958, 1986, 1991 by the Trustees for the e.e. Cummings Trust, from *Complete Poems: 1904-1962* by e. e. Cummings. Edited by George J. Firmage. Reprinted by permission of Liveright Publishing Corporation.

de Burgos, Julia. "To Julia de Burgos." Translated by Maria Arrillaga, 1971.

Dickinson, Emily. (#465) "I Heard a Fly Buzz" and (#986) "A narrow Fellow in the Grass" from *The Poems of Emily Dickinson*. Edited by Thomas H. Johnson, Cambridge, Mass.: The Belknap Press of Harvard University Press. Copyright © 1951, 1955, 1979, 1983 by the President and Fellows of Harvard College. Reprinted by permission of the publishers and the Trustees of Amherst College.

Espada, Martín. "Tiburón" from *Trumpets from the Islands of Their Eviction, Expanded Edition* by Martín Espada. Copyright © 1994 by Bilingual Press/Editorial Bilingüe. Reprinted by permission of Bilingual Press/Editorial Bilingüe, Arizona State University, Tempe, AZ.

Frost, Robert. "Birches" from *The Poetry of Robert Frost*. Edited by Edward Connery Lathem. Copyright 1944, 1951 by Robert Frost. Copyright 1916, 1923, © 1969 by Henry Holt and Company, Inc. © 1997 by Edward Connery Lathem. Reprinted by permission of Henry Holt and Company, Inc.

Gibson, Wilfrid Wilson. "Flannan Isle." Reprinted by permission of Macmillan.

Hollander, John. "Swan and Shadow" from *Types of Shape* by John Hollander. Reprinted by permission of Yale University Press.

Ignatow, David. "Two Friends" from *Figure of the Human* by David Ignatow. © 1964 by David Ignatow, Wesleyan University Press. Reprinted by permission of the University Press of New England.

Justice, Donald. "Poem to Be Read at 3 A.M." from *New And Selected Poems* by Donald Justice. Copyright © 1995 by Donald Justice. Reprinted by permission of Alfred A. Knopf, Inc.

Kooser, Ted. "Abandoned Farmhouse" from *Sure Signs: New And Selected Poems*, by Ted Kooser. Reprinted by permission of the University of Pittsburgh Press. © 1980 by Ted Kooser.

Levertov, Denise. "The Breathing" from *Poems 1960-1967*. Copyright © 1966 by Denise Levertov. Reprinted by permission of New Directions Publishing Corporation.

Levine, Philip. "When I Hear Your Name" by Gloria Fuertes. Translated by Philip Levine from *Off The Map*, Wesleyan University Press. Reprinted by permission of Philip Levine.

Madgett, Naomi Long. "Woman with Flower" from *Star by Star* by Naomi Long Madgett. Reprinted by permission of the author.

Mark, Diane Mei Lin. "Rice and Rose Bowl Blues." Reprinted by permission of the author.

Masefield, John. "Cargoes." Reprinted by permission of The Society of Authors as the Literary Representative of the Estate of John Masefield.

Masters, Marcia. "April" from *Contemporary Poetry*, Winter 1994. Reprinted by permission of Marcia Cavell.

Merriam, Eve. "Metaphor" from *A Sky Full of Poems* by Eve Merriam. Copyright © 1964, 1970, 1973 by Eve Merriam. Reprinted by permission of Marian Reiner.

Mitsui, James Masao. "The Morning My Father Died" from *Journal of the Sun* by James Masao Mitsui. Reprinted by permission of the author.

Momaday, N. Scott. "The Burning." Copyright © N. Scott Momaday. Reprinted by permission of the author.

Moses, Daniel David. "The Corn." First published in *Whetstone*, Spring, 1985.

Nye, Naomi Shihab. "The Flying Cat" from *Hugging the Jukebox* by Naomi Shihab Nye. Reprinted by permission of the author.

Piercy, Marge. "A Work of Artifice from *Circles On The Water* by Marge Piercy. Copyright © 1982 by Marge Piercy. Reprinted by permission of Alfred A. Knopf, Inc.

Reed, Ishmael. ".05" from *Chattanooga* by Ishmael Reed. Copyright © 1973 by Ishmael Reed. Reprinted by permission.

continued on page 260

CONTENTS

TO THE STUDENT

> "She walks in Beauty, like the night/Of cloudless climes and starry skies;"
>
> "Shall I compare thee to a summer's day?/Thou art more lovely and more temperate:"
>
> "Come, my friends,/'Tis not too late to seek a newer world."
>
> "Once upon a midnight dreary, while I pondered, weak and weary,"
>
> "Like men we'll face the murderous, cowardly pack,/Pressed to the wall, dying, but fighting back!"

In this book you will read the poems which first introduced these unforgettable lines to the world. Although you will not remember every line of every poem, if you are like most people certain lines will lodge themselves in your memory—perhaps for the rest of your life. Years from now you will still be able to recall and enjoy their unique sounds, images, and meanings.

What makes poems so affecting and so memorable? First and foremost, poets love words and they understand the power of both their sounds and their meanings. Using just the right words, poets are able to compact large ideas about such topics as life, love, and death into a few short lines. In the best poems these words ring so true that they become part of a reader's memory forever.

Because poems pack a great deal of meaning into a few words, they often can be dense and complex. There almost seems to be a code that you need to crack before you can understand them thoroughly. In this book you will get the help you need to understand poetry. Not every poem that you read will be explained in detail. It would be foolish to attempt such as task, since in many cases the meaning of a poem depends upon the interpretation of the person reading it. Instead of trying to analyze every poem, this book focuses on specific elements that are outstanding in each poem. By completing the lessons in this book, you will gain experience in recognizing and appreciating the elements that make a poem superior. You will analyze the techniques that poets use to create their work, and you will have the opportunity to try those techniques in poems that you write yourself.

UNIT FORMAT AND ACTIVITIES

- Each unit begins with a list of all the poems you will read in that unit. About the Lessons explains why the poems are grouped the way they are. In general, poems are grouped together because they are particularly good examples of one element of poetry that will be taught in that unit.
- The unit's major writing exercise is then introduced. In this exercise you will begin planning for the writing project that you will complete at the end of the unit. Periodically throughout the unit, you will have opportunities to explore and develop ideas for your writing project.
- About This Poet focuses on one important poet whose work appears in that unit. Here you will learn about the poet's life, major accomplishments, and works.
- Next, there are questions for you to ask yourself as you read the poems in the unit.
- The poems themselves make up the next section. Before each poem is a short biography of the poet and/or further information about the poem. These notes have been included because knowing something about a poet and the poem's content may help you better understand and appreciate the work.
- Following the poems are questions that test your comprehension and critical thinking skills. Your answers to these questions and to other exercises in the unit should be recorded in a personal literature notebook. You also should check your answers with your teacher.
- Your teacher may provide you with charts to record your progress in developing your comprehension skills: The Comprehension Skills Graph *records* your scores and the

Comprehension Skills Profile *analyzes* your scores—providing you with information about the skills on which you need to focus. You can talk with your teacher about ways to work on those comprehension skills.

- The next section contains two or three lessons, which begin with a discussion of the literary concept that is the unit's focus. Each lesson illustrates one or more techniques that poets use to develop the concept. For example, you will see how a poet uses sensory details and concrete language to create memorable images.
- Short-answer exercises test your understanding of the poets' techniques as illustrated in particular poems that appear in the unit. You can check your answers to the exercises with your teacher and determine what you need to review.
- Each lesson also includes a writing exercise that guides you in creating your own original work using the techniques you have just studied.
- Discussion guides and a final writing activity round out each unit in the book. These activities will help sharpen your reading, thinking, speaking, and writing skills.
- At the back of the book is a discussion of the writing process. You may want to refer to it as you complete your writing exercises and projects. You also will find a glossary of literary terms. You can refer to the glossary when you encounter an unfamiliar term or concept.

Reading the poems in this book will enable you to recognize and appreciate the skills it takes to write a good poem. When you understand what makes a poem good, you will be better able to choose and enjoy worthwhile poems on your own. The writing exercises will help you become a better writer by giving you practice in using other poets' techniques to make your own poetry more effective and appealing.

What Is a Poem?

Flying Fish
by Carl Sandburg

Self Portrait
by Samantha Abeel

The Argument of His Book
by Robert Herrick

April
by Marcia Masters

.05
by Ishmael Reed

old age sticks
by e. e. cummings

Birches
by Robert Frost

I Am Singing Now
by Luci Tapahonso

INTRODUCTION

ABOUT THE LESSONS

Long before people had systems of writing, they often shared stories by reciting them in the form of poetry. Long after writing was invented, people wrote stories in the form of poetry rather than in conversational language. Only in the last few hundred years have some people chosen to write in prose instead of poetry, using sentences and paragraphs instead of lines and stanzas.

Why is it that so many imaginative people have chosen to present their ideas in the form of poetry? Why are poems so powerful? In this unit you will consider these questions as you look at some elements that are common to most poems. The lessons will look at these characteristics: 1) poets find meaning or raise questions as they experience the world around them, and then they relate those experiences or questions to others; 2) poets distinguish their messages from normal, everyday communication by using special sounds, patterns, and forms; 3) poets use imagery, striking comparisons, and exact detail to make their messages vivid and memorable. Each of the three groups of poems in this unit highlights one of these characteristics.

WRITING: DEVELOPING A POET'S EYE AND EAR

Not every writer sits down with the express purpose of writing a poem. In fact, you already may have written a poem without knowing it. That is because everyday speech contains rhythm, rhyme, and the repetition of sounds. People naturally fill their conversations with ear-catching sounds, interesting comparisons, and humorous wordplay. At the end of this unit you will write a poem, using your natural speech patterns along with other poetic elements. For now, begin to develop a poet's eye and ear with these suggestions:

- Sometimes people use poetic language without thinking. For example, writing that is intended to serve a special purpose, such as signs and labels, often has a rhythm and a form that suggest poetry. Because these poems are found by chance, they are called *found poems.* For one day, carry a notebook with you and look for found poems in signs that you see in school or on the street or on labels that you read on cans or bottles. Look for signs whose lines break in ways that suggest a poem. You are the judge of what constitutes a found poem. Here is one example:

Fair Warning!
Trespassers will be
prosecuted to the
full extent of the law!

- For one day, listen to the natural speech of everyone around you—your friends, your teachers, your family, radio announcers, and television actors. Do you hear any rhymes? repetition of sounds and words? obvious rhythms in speech? unusual comparisons or descriptions? In your notebook record any interesting uses of sounds and words.

ABOUT THIS POET

Carl Sandburg (1878–1967) was a historian, a biographer, and one of the most important modern poets in the United States. In all his works he showed an enthusiasm toward the American way of life and the common man. Sandburg was born in Galesburg, Illinois, and left school at age 13 to take on a series of jobs. As a young man he traveled about as a hobo, and then in 1898, he served briefly in the U.S. Army during the Spanish-American War. Later that year he returned home to study at Lombard College in Galesburg. In 1902 he dropped out. He then worked for the Socialist Party in Wisconsin for about 10 years.

From 1912 through the 1920s Sandburg worked as a newspaper writer, primarily in Chicago. During that time he established his reputation as a poet with the publication of *Chicago Poems* (1916) and a series of other collections. He and other important writers living in Chicago then became known as the *Chicago School*.

In 1926 he published the first two volumes of his biography of Abraham Lincoln, called *Abraham Lincoln: The Prairie Years*. Its success allowed him to concentrate on literature. Earlier he had begun collecting American folktales, ballads, and other folklore. In 1927 he published his collection of folk songs in *The American Songbag*. His study of folklore also influenced much of his poetry and the books he wrote for children, such as *The Rootabaga Stories* (1922).

In the 1930s Sandburg published *The People, Yes* (1936)—a long poem that included American folktale heroes—and the last four volumes of his Lincoln biography, *Abraham Lincoln: The War Years* (1939). The biography earned him the 1940 Pulitzer Prize for history. In 1951 he won the Pulitzer Prize for poetry for his *Collected Poems* (1950). Sandburg, like Walt Whitman, wanted to speak for the American people. In many ways he achieved that goal.

AS YOU READ

As you read each poem in this unit, ask yourself these questions:

- Who is speaking in this poem? What message is the speaker expressing, and why?
- What sounds and sound patterns do I find in the poem that I don't hear in normal conversation or see in prose writing?
- What pictures does the poem paint in my mind?

Flying Fish

by Carl Sandburg

ABOUT THE SELECTION

Carl Sandburg (1878–1967) was one of the most important modern poets in the United States. He traveled widely and held a series of jobs before becoming a journalist in Chicago. When his first book of poetry was published in 1916, he became nationally known and eventually won two Pulitzer Prizes. For more information about Sandburg, see About This Poet at the beginning of this unit. Perhaps "Flying Fish" reflects Sandburg's feelings during some of his early travels.

I have lived in many half-worlds myself . . . and so
    I know you.

I leaned at a deck rail watching a monotonous sea,
    the same circling birds and the same plunge
    of furrows[1] carved by the plowing keel.

I leaned so . . . and you fluttered struggling between
    two waves in the air now . . . and then under the water
    and out again . . . a fish . . . a bird . . . a fin thing . . .
    a wing thing.

Child of water, child of air, fin thing and wing thing . . .
    I have lived in many half-worlds myself . . .
    and so I know you.

---

[1] long, shallow trenches or grooves

Self Portrait

by Samantha Abeel

ABOUT THE SELECTION

When Samantha Abeel (1977–) was in seventh grade, she learned that she had a learning disability. In order to prove to herself and others that she had strengths as well as weaknesses, she began writing poetry. Her first book of poems, *Reach for the Moon*, was published while she was still in high school. "Self Portrait" is from that collection.

To show you who I am
I crawled inside a tree, became its roots, bark and leaves,
listened to its whispers in the wind.
When fall came and painted the leaves red and gold
I wanted to shake them across your lawn
to transform the grass into a quilt, a gift spread at your feet,
but their numbers eluded[1] me,
so I turned a piece of paper into my soul
to send to you so that you might see
how easily it can be crumpled and flattened out again.
I wanted you to see my resilience,[2]
but I wasn't sure how to arrange the numbers in your address,
so I danced with the Indians in the forest
and collected the feathers that fell from the eagle's wings,
each one a wish for my future,
but I lost track of their numbers, gathered too many,
and was unable to carry them home

---

[1] escaped from, as by skill

[2] ability to recover quickly from illness or other setback

so I reaped the wind with my hair,
relived its journey through my senses, and
felt its whispered loneliness, like lakes in winter,
but it was too far and you could not follow me.

Now I've written out their shadows
like the wind collects its secrets
to whisper into receptive ears, and I
will leave them at your doorstep,
a reminder of what others cannot see,
a reminder of what I can and cannot be.

The Argument of His Book

by Robert Herrick

ABOUT THE SELECTION

Robert Herrick (1591–1674), the vicar of a rural church, produced some of England's finest lyric poems. Born in London, Herrick was ordained a minister in the Church of England in 1621. He served in a small parish in Devonshire (now Devon). Although his poems were not published until 1648 they were already popular, having circulated widely in manuscript form. Many of his best works are love poems to imaginary women and poems about nature and country life, such as "The Argument of His Book." In this poem Herrick uses the term *argument* to mean "summary, or short statement of subject matter."

I sing of brooks, of blossoms, birds and bowers,[1]
Of April, May, of June and Jùly-flowers;
I sing of May-poles, hock-carts, wassails,[2] wakes,
Of bridegrooms, brides and of their bridal cakes;
I write of youth, of love, and have access
By these to sing of cleanly wantonness;[3]
I sing of dews, of rains, and piece by piece
Of balm, of oil, of spice and ambergris;[4]
I sing of times trans-shifting, and I write
How roses first came red and lilies white;
I write of groves, of twilights, and I sing
The Court of Mab,[5] and of the Fairy King;
I write of hell; I sing (and ever shall)
Of heaven, and hope to have it after all.

---

[1] shady resting places in a garden
[2] festive occasions marked by drinking
[3] playfulness
[4] waxy substance added to perfumes to slow down evaporation
[5] queen of the fairies

April

by Marcia Masters

ABOUT THE SELECTION

The scene that Marcia Masters paints in "April" is of a world long gone, before television and cars provided easy access to entertainments away from the neighborhoods people lived in. Try to put yourself in this scene, on a street full of children as late afternoon turns into evening.

It's lemonade, it's lemonade, it's daisy.
It's a roller-skating, scissor-grinding day;
It's gingham-waisted,[1] chocolate flavored, lazy,
With the children flower-scattered at their play.

It's the sun like watermelon,
And the sidewalks overlaid
With a glaze of yellow yellow
Like a jar of marmalade.

It's the mower gently mowing,
And the stars like startled glass,
While the mower keeps on going
Through a waterfall of grass.

Then the rich magenta[2] evening
Like a sauce upon the walk,
And the porches softly swinging
With a hammockful of talk.

---

[1] referring to dresses made of a cloth whose patterns are usually checks, plaids, or stripes

[2] purplish-red

It's the hobo at the corner
With his lilac-sniffing gait,
And the shy departing thunder
Of the fast departing skate.

It's lemonade, it's lemonade, it's April!
A water sprinkler, puddle winking time,
When a boy who peddles slowly, with a smile remote and holy,
Sells you April chocolate flavored for a dime.

.05

by Ishmael Reed

ABOUT THE SELECTION

Ishmael Reed (1938–), is a controversial and major figure in today's African American literature. He has written that he was "born in Chattanooga, Tennessee, grew up in Buffalo, New York, learned to write in New York City and wised up in Berkeley, California." In 1967 he began teaching at the University of California at Berkeley and has since taught at several other universities. He has stated, "Whether I've written plays, novels, poetry, articles, or lyrics, the main purpose of my work has been to serve the underdog and to side with those who are suffering injustice." The poem ".05" reflects Reed's biting humor.

If i had a nickel
For all the women who've
Rejected me in my life
I would be the head of the
World Bank with a flunkie
To hold my derby as i
Prepared to fly chartered
Jet to sign a check
Giving India a new lease
On life

If i had a nickel for
All the women who've loved
Me in my life i would be
The World Bank's assistant
Janitor and wouldn't need
To wear a derby
All i'd think about would
Be going home

old age sticks

by e. e. cummings

ABOUT THE SELECTION

Edward Estlin Cummings (1894–1962), who signed his works e. e. cummings, wrote poems noted for their original capitalization and punctuation, the unusual ways their words are divided and arranged on paper, and the forcefulness with which they express themes. Cummings was born in Cambridge, Massachusetts, graduated from Harvard University, and drove an ambulance in France during World War I. There, by error, he was charged with treason and held in a detention camp for six months. After the war, Cummings was successful both as a poet and a painter. The poem "old age sticks" indicates his imaginative way of looking at the "generation gap."

old age sticks
up Keep
Off
signs)&

youth yanks them
down(old
age
cries No

Tres)&(pas)
youth laughs
(sing
old age
scolds Forbid
den Stop
Must
n't Don't

&)youth goes
right on
gr
owing old

Birches

by Robert Frost

ABOUT THE SELECTION

Robert Frost (1874–1963), winner of four Pulitzer Prizes, was a farmer in New England for about 10 years before establishing his fame as a poet. Although he was not very successful as a farmer, his experiences during this time gave him much valuable material for his poems. The insightful way he describes the trees in "Birches" proves that he spent a great deal of time studying nature and humans' relationship to it.

When I see birches bend to left and right
Across the line of straighter darker trees,
I like to think some boy's been swinging them.
But swinging doesn't bend them down to stay.
Ice-storms do that. Often you must have seen them
Loaded with ice a sunny winter morning
After a rain. They click upon themselves
As the breeze rises, and turn many-colored
As the stir cracks and crazes their enamel.
Soon the sun's warmth makes them shed crystal shells
Shattering and avalanching on the snow-crust—
Such heaps of broken glass to sweep away
You'd think the inner dome of heaven had fallen.
They are dragged to the withered bracken by the load,
And they seem not to break; though once they are bowed
So low for long, they never right themselves:
You may see their trunks arching in the woods
Years afterwards, trailing their leaves on the ground

Like girls on hands and knees that throw their hair
Before them over their heads to dry in the sun.
But I was going to say when Truth broke in
With all her matter-of-fact about the ice-storm
I should prefer to have some boy bend them
As he went out and in to fetch the cows—
Some boy too far from town to learn baseball,
Whose only play was what he found himself,
Summer or winter, and could play alone.
One by one he subdued his father's trees
By riding them down over and over again
Until he took the stiffness out of them,
And not one but hung limp, not one was left
For him to conquer. He learned all there was
To learn about not launching out too soon
And so not carrying the tree away
Clear to the ground. He always kept his poise
To the top branches, climbing carefully
With the same pains you use to fill a cup
Up to the brim, and even above the brim.
Then he flung outward, feet first, with a swish,
Kicking his way down through the air to the ground.

So was I once myself a swinger of birches;
And so I dream of going back to be.
It's when I'm weary of considerations,
And life is too much like a pathless wood
Where your face burns and tickles with the cobwebs
Broken across it, and one eye is weeping
From a twig's having lashed across it open.
I'd like to get away from earth awhile
And then come back to it and begin over.
May no fate willfully misunderstand me
And half grant what I wish and snatch me away
Not to return. Earth's the right place for love:
I don't know where it's likely to go better.

I'd like to go by climbing a birch tree,
And climb black branches up a snow-white trunk
Toward heaven, till the tree could bear no more,
But dipped its top and set me down again.
That would be good both going and coming back.
One could do worse than be a swinger of birches.

I Am Singing Now

by Luci Tapahonso

ABOUT THE SELECTION

Luci Tapahonso (1953–) is a Navajo poet from Shiprock, New Mexico. She was raised within the Navajo culture. She earned both her bachelor's and master's degrees from the University of New Mexico and has taught English there and at the University of Kansas, Lawrence. Her books of poetry reflect her deep interest and pride in the Navajo way of life. In this poem look for the loving way in which she describes the landscape of her home.

the moon is a white sliver
balancing the last of its contents
in the final curve of the month

my daughters sleep
in the back of the pickup
breathing small clouds of white in the dark
they lie warm and soft
under layers of clothes and blankets
how they dream, precious ones, of grandma
and the scent of fire
the smell of mutton
they are already home

i watch the miles dissolve behind us
in the hazy glow of taillights and
the distinct shape of hills and mesas loom above
then recede slowly in the clear winter night.

i sing to myself and
think of my father
teaching me, leaning towards me
listening as i learned.
"just like this," he would say
and he would sing those old songs

into the fiber of my hair,
into the pores of my skin,
into the dreams of my children

and i am singing now
for the night
the almost empty moon
and the land swimming beneath cold bright stars.

UNDERSTANDING THE POEMS

Record your answers to these questions in your personal literature notebook. Follow the directions for each group.

GROUP 1

Reread the poems in Group 1 to complete these sentences.

Reviewing the Selection

1. The speaker in "Flying Fish" sees the fish when he or she is
   a. fishing.
   b. preparing fish for dinner.
   c. dreaming.
   d. traveling on a ship.

Interpreting the Selection

2. In saying "I have lived in many half-worlds myself," the speaker in "Flying Fish" means that he or she
   a. is usually only half-awake every day.
   b. often feels not fully part of the world around him or her.
   c. feels that half of what he or she has done in life was not worth doing.
   d. gets out of the world only half of what he or she expects from it.

3. "Self Portrait" describes
   a. why the speaker writes poems.
   b. imaginary adventures the speaker has had.
   c. what the speaker thinks about things in a forest.
   d. what the speaker looks like.

Recognizing How Words Are Used

4. In line 1 of "The Argument of His Book" the poet could have used the phrase *shady places* instead of the word *bowers.* Of the following considerations, the one that is *not* a valid reason for choosing *bowers* is to
   a. repeat beginning sounds.
   b. rhyme with *flowers.*
   c. name a place.
   d. match the number of accented syllables in line 2.

Appreciating Poetry

5. One characteristic that all three of the poems in Group 1 share is that
- a. they all use rhyme.
- b. all three poems include words that are no longer commonly in use.
- c. the speaker in each poem tells about himself or herself.
- d. the mood of each poem is sad.

GROUP 2

Reread the poems in Group 2 to complete these sentences.

Reviewing the Selection

6. The only colorful object below that is not mentioned in "April" is a
- a. jar of yellow marmalade.
- b. watermelon-red sun.
- c. yellow, checked dress.
- d. magenta sunset.

7. The poem "old age sticks" discusses
- a. an old man and a youth.
- b. signs posted around a home for the elderly.
- c. young people who tear down signs that older people put up.
- d. advice that older people give but that younger people ignore.

Interpreting the Selection

8. The speaker in ".05" is complaining about
- a. his job as an assistant janitor.
- b. not having enough money.
- c. not having enough girlfriends who feel strongly about him.
- d. not getting any respect in his job.

Recognizing How Words Are Used

9. In "April" the phrase "a waterfall of grass" suggests that
- a. so much grass is flying from the mower that it looks like a waterfall.
- b. the sprinkler is pouring so much water onto the grass that the water looks like a waterfall.
- c. the grass is so tall that it bends over and looks like a waterfall.
- d. the mower runs over a sprinkler, which creates a waterfall effect.

Appreciating Poetry

10. The tone of ".05" is best described as
a. sad.
b. cheerful.
c. hopeful.
d. preachy.

GROUP 3

Reread the poems in Group 3 to complete these sentences.

Reviewing the Selection

11. The speaker in "Birches" likes to think that the trees were bent low by
a. a boy who was looking for some fun.
b. a heavy ice storm.
c. a windstorm that recently passed through.
d. the warmth of the sun.

12. The speaker in "I Am Singing Now" is
a. trying to find the way through a desert.
b. learning how to sing an ancient song.
c. driving on a winter night.
d. swimming under cold, bright stars.

Interpreting the Selection

13. The speaker in "I Am Singing Now" is feeling comfortable and cheerful for all these reasons *except* that
a. the miles are passing quickly.
b. it is a cold, clear night.
c. his or her daughters are at home waiting.
d. he or she is recalling feeling close to his or her father.

Recognizing How Words Are Used

14. In "Birches" ice that has fallen from the branches of birches is compared to
a. a girl's hair thrown before her.
b. heaps of broken glass.
c. lights in a pathless wood.
d. ice-cream cones.

Appreciating Poetry

15. The mood of "I Am Singing Now" could be described as
 a. contented.
 b. lonely.
 c. stressful.
 d. anxious.

Now check your answers with your teacher. Study the questions you answered incorrectly. What types of questions were they? Talk with your teacher about ways to work on those skills.

What Is a Poem?

According to the dictionary, a poet is not only a writer of poems but also a person who demonstrates keen insight and a vivid imagination. From this we can suppose that insightfulness and imagination are major characteristics of a poem. How are these characteristics expressed differently in poetry than in prose? The lessons in this unit will focus on these ways:

1. Most poets relate experiences in ways that are meaningful to others as well as to the poets themselves. To relate specific experiences or messages most effectively, poets choose their speakers carefully.
2. Poets use sounds and sound patterns to increase the impact of their words. Some poets also give their poems distinctive appearances.
3. Poets often express their feelings and thoughts through images that they create with specific, concrete language and surprising comparisons.

LESSON 1

SPEAKER AND MESSAGE

Sometimes the message of a poem is stated directly and clearly, and the person we hear speaking is unmistakably the poet. For example, in "The Argument of His Book" Robert Herrick, a cheerful minister, speaks through the poem to let potential readers know what they will find in his book of poetry:

> I sing of brooks, of blossoms, birds and bowers,
> Of April, May, of June and Jùly-flowers;
> I sing of May-poles, hock-carts, wassails, wakes,
> Of bridegrooms, brides and of their bridal cakes;
> I write of youth, of love, and have access
> By these to sing of cleanly wantonness;
> . . .
> I write of hell; I sing (and ever shall)
> Of heaven, and hope to have it after all.

However, such directness and clarity are not found in every poem. Sometimes we readers have to puzzle out the message. We might even have a tough time identifying the speaker. Actually, we should not be surprised that this happens. A poet often intentionally describes unusual situations and uses unexpected comparisons to force us to slow down and think about what we are reading. The poet has stumbled upon a truth or discovered a lesson that was not obvious to him or her and wants us to experience the same thrill of discovery.

If the poem were immediately understood, the message would have much less of an impact. Notice, for example, what happens in Samantha Abeel's "Self Portrait." The very first line identifies the speaker's goal: "To show you who I am." But the process of identifying and communicating "who I am" is not an easy matter. The next 20 lines of the poem lead readers through an imaginative and dizzying series of transformations as the speaker tries one approach after another:

> I crawled inside a tree, became its roots, bark and leaves, . . .
>
> so I turned a piece of paper into my soul . . .
>
> so I danced with the Indians in the forest . . .
>
> so I reaped the wind with my hair,
> relived its journey through my senses, and
> felt its whispered loneliness, . . .

But each transformation ends with dissatisfaction and the speaker sensing that nothing quite does the job:

> but their numbers eluded me, . . .
>
> but I wasn't sure how to arrange the numbers in your address, . . .
>
> but I lost track of their numbers, gathered too many,
>
> and was unable to carry them home . . .
>
> but it was too far and you could not follow me.

At last the speaker comes upon a way to express what he or she has learned. This approach, too, is imperfect, but perhaps part of what the speaker has learned is that not even he or she will ever know all there is to know about himself or herself.

> Now I've written out their shadows
> like the wind collects its secrets
> to whisper into receptive ears, and I
> will leave them at your doorstep,
> a reminder of what others cannot see,
> a reminder of what I can and cannot be.

EXERCISE 1

Reread the poem "Flying Fish." Then use what you have learned in this lesson to answer these questions:

1. Where is the speaker in "Flying Fish"? What is he or she doing? To whom or what is he or she speaking?
2. What similarity does the speaker find between himself or herself and the one to whom he or she is speaking?

Now check your answers with your teacher. Review this part of the lesson if you don't understand why an answer was incorrect.

WRITING ON YOUR OWN 

In this lesson you examined the poem "Self Portrait." At the end of this unit you will write a poem that is your own self-portrait. Begin the plan for your poem by doing some self-evaluation. Follow these steps:

- List at least three qualities or characteristics for which you would like to be known. They need not be qualities that you

have already developed; they could represent your ideals. For example, if you are trying to develop patience, you could list it as one of your qualities even though it isn't fully developed.
- Next, list at least three qualities or characteristics that your worst enemy would point out in you.
- Last, list at least three qualities or characteristics that you can honestly say you have now. They may or may not be praiseworthy, but they should be the qualities or characteristics that close acquaintances would recognize in you. If you'd like, you can ask your friends for their opinions.
- Save your list to use in later writing exercises.

SOUND AND FORM

Within the last 150 years, poets writing in English have used less traditional forms of poetry than were used before. Traditional poetry has set rules about the patterns of stressed syllables in lines and the patterns of rhyme in a stanza. Nontraditional poetry pays little, if any, attention to these rules. At the same time, however, some nontraditional poems put a great deal more emphasis on appearance than traditional poems do. Both types of poems do have this much in common: They are written in lines grouped in stanzas, as opposed to sentences grouped in paragraphs. Further, patterns of sounds are important in both, adding emphasis to the words and pleasure to reading them.

"April" is an example of a traditional poem. Notice that every stanza has the same number of lines. The poem uses patterns of repeated sounds, both at the beginning of words and at the ending. The use of the same consonant sounds in words that are close together is called *alliteration*. An example is the /s/ sound in "stars like startled glass." The use of the same sounds at the end of two words is called *rhyme*. An example of two rhyming words in the poem is *glass* and *grass*. In each stanza of "April," the second and fourth lines end in rhyming words; in most stanzas, the first and third lines also end in words that rhyme or almost rhyme, for example:

It's the mower gently mowing,
And the stars like startled glass,
While the mower keeps on going
Through a waterfall of grass.

In addition to patterns of repeated sounds, in "April" there are easily distinguishable patterns of stressed and unstressed syllables, which are called *rhythms*. Reread the above stanza to yourself—preferably aloud. By the time you have completed the stanza, you should be able to match its rhythmic pattern to one of the two examples below:

A	B
da da DA da DA da DA da	da DA da DA da DA da DA da DA da
da da DA da DA da DA	da DA da DA da DA da DA da DA
da da DA da DA da DA da	da DA da DA da DA da DA da DA da
da da DA da DA da DA	da DA da DA da DA da DA da DA

Now look at ".05" again. Both the appearance and the sound of this poem are less regular and traditional than "April." The two stanzas in ".05" are of different lengths, and the lines are not linked by rhyming or repeated sounds. In fact, lines that are grouped like these are sometimes called *verse paragraphs* instead of stanzas because they are grouped like a prose paragraph and not according to a rhyme pattern. A verse paragraph can be longer or shorter than other verse paragraphs in the same poem; rather than relying on a particular pattern or formula, it uses as many lines as are required to convey the main idea.

Compare the conversational, irregular pattern of ".05" with the strong and regular rhythm of "April." In ".05" it would be difficult to find any two lines with the same pattern of stressed and unstressed syllables. Yet even in this nontraditional poem—which is called a *free verse*—there is a repetition of sounds that gives it structure. Notice that each stanza, or verse paragraph, begins with the phrase *If i had a nickel* and includes *me in my life*, *World Bank*, and *derby*. Although the stanzas are of different lengths, the fact that stanza 2 repeats words as it contrasts ideas gives a balance to the two parts.

Notice also that ".05" uses nonstandard capitalization and punctuation as a means of making the appearance of the poem distinctive, but that this technique does not affect the poem's meaning. You still would be able to understand the poem even if you couldn't see it. By contrast, to appreciate "old age sticks" you could not simply hear the poem; you also must see it. Note how the parentheses set off the words that relate to what old age says, separating them from youth's reaction. If you wanted to, you could read the old-age part of the poem first and then go back and read the poem again for the part about youth. In the lines below the "old age" part is underlined:

youth yanks them
down(old
age
cries No

Tres)&(pas)
youth laughs
(sing
old age

scolds Forbid
den Stop
Must
n't Don't

In more modern poetry when a poet is confident that readers will see a poem in print, they often rely on the poem's appearance rather than its sound to give it shape and intensify its meaning.

EXERCISE 2

Reread "April" and then use what you have learned in this lesson to answer these questions:

1. Compare all the stanzas in "April" with the two metrical patterns in this lesson that are labeled *A* and *B.* Which of the stanzas match pattern *A?* Which are closer to pattern *B?*

2. Sometimes alliteration occurs only at the beginnings of words, as in the /st/ sound in the phrase *stars like startled glass.* At other times alliteration occurs anywhere in words, as in the /s/ sound in the same phrase: *stars like startled glass.* In the second stanza of "April" identify all the words in which the /s/ sound occurs anywhere in the word. Then identify all the words in which the /l/ sound occurs anywhere.

Now check your answers with your teacher. Review this part of the lesson if you don't understand why an answer was incorrect.

WRITING ON YOUR OWN 

In this lesson you have studied some of the differences between traditional and nontraditional poetry. In this exercise you will practice writing both types of poetry. Follow these steps:

- Review the lists of personal qualities or characteristics that you made for Writing on Your Own 1 and choose one of them. Then write two to four lines of nontraditional or free-verse poetry about that quality or characteristic and how it does or does not describe you. The lines should be unrhymed, with no regular rhythm, and the lines can vary in length. Write your complete thoughts, but you need not use traditional capitalization or punctuation.
- Now choose a different quality or characteristic from your lists or reuse the one you just wrote about in the nontraditional poem.

This time, write a two- to four-line traditional poem about the quality or characteristic. At least two of the lines must rhyme. Make the rhythm of the lines as regular as possible.

- Save your work for the final writing exercise in this unit.

LESSON 3 IMAGERY

Just as a painter uses paints and a canvas to create a picture, or an image, poets create imagery with words. The most common kind is *visual imagery*—that is, imagery that appeals to your sense of sight. For example, a poet may describe a sunset, giving details about the colors of the sun and sky or the shapes of the clouds. But poets also create imagery that appeals to other senses and helps readers recreate not only how things look but also how they smell, taste, sound, and feel. Because these descriptions appeal to all the senses, they are called *sensory images*.

In "I Am Singing Now" Luci Tapahonso recreates a moment in time by introducing a variety of sensory images. The poem begins with a visual image of the moon:

> the moon is a white sliver
> balancing the last of its contents
> in the final curve of the month

Next, the poem appeals to other senses with a series of comforting images:

> my daughters sleep
> in the back of the pickup
> breathing small clouds of white in the dark
> they lie warm and soft
> under layers of clothes and blankets
> how they dream, precious ones, of grandma
>   and the scent of fire
>   the smell of mutton

As you read, you can feel the cold that causes the "small clouds of white" from the children's breath as well as the warmth, softness, and weight of the layers of clothes and blankets. You also can smell the fire and the mutton that is cooking. All of these details together create images that draw you into the experience as if you were there.

Notice how the form of this poem works together with its images. The first set of lines about the moon is placed on the right side of the page like a moon shining down on the speaker. The other verse paragraphs are arranged in a zigzag form, perhaps to suggest driving down a winding road.

As you have just seen, poets often try to recreate feelings and experiences in an almost photographic, concrete way. They also, however, like to look at the world from an unusual viewpoint and then combine and compare images that you would not normally connect. In this way, they help you appreciate and better understand parts of life that you sometimes might take for granted. For example, read this excerpt from "Birches" by Robert Frost to see the comparisons that the speaker makes while looking at the ice-covered branches of birch trees.

> . . . Often you must have seen them
> Loaded with ice a sunny winter morning
> After a rain. They click upon themselves
> As the breeze rises, and turn many-colored
> As the stir cracks and crazes their enamel.
> Soon the sun's warmth makes them shed crystal shells
> Shattering and avalanching on the snow-crust—
> Such heaps of broken glass to sweep away
> You'd think the inner dome of heaven had fallen.

The speaker compares ice to enamel, crystal shells, and broken glass from the dome of heaven. Not everyone would make the same comparisons, but when you think about them, they make sense. When you first read them, you might have found yourself saying, "I'd never thought about ice like that before, but

I understand and agree with the comparison." That is part of the poet's artistry—to take a piece of reality and serve it up to readers in a new and thought-provoking way.

EXERCISE 

Reread the poems in Group 3 and then use what you have learned in this lesson to answer these questions:

1. In "Birches" to what does the speaker compare trees that are bent low for so long that they never completely right themselves?
2. Identify five sensory images in "I Am Singing Now" and classify each one as appealing to the sense of sight, smell, touch, taste, or hearing.

Now check your answers with your teacher. Review this part of the lesson if you don't understand why an answer was incorrect.

WRITING ON YOUR OWN 

This lesson focused on the importance of sensory images and comparisons in poems. Now you can make your self-portrait vivid with both of these techniques. Follow these steps:

- Choose one or two physical characteristics that you would like to mention in your poem. Write a sentence about each, using precise descriptive words.
- Now compare yourself to a nonhuman thing. Consider each of these questions: If you were a plant, what kind of plant would you be? If you were a place of business—office, store, factory, wherever people work—what kind would you be? If you were a piece of furniture, what kind would you be? For each question, write one or two sentences that tell not only the answer but the reasoning behind your choice.
- Save your work for the final writing exercise in this unit.

DISCUSSION GUIDES

1. How do you feel about poetry? What do you like or dislike about this form of writing? If you have free time for reading, which type of writing would you be more likely to choose—a short story or a poem? Can you think of or quote from a favorite poem? What elements of poetry mentioned in this unit's overview sound the most interesting to you? After discussing these questions with your classmates, work together to draw up a questionnaire containing three to five questions about people's attitudes toward poetry. Make sure your questions can be answered with the word *yes* or *no* or with a number from 1 to 10. Have everyone in the class answer the questionnaire and then tabulate the results. Save the questionnaire until you finish this book. Then issue the questionnaire a second time to see if anyone's attitude toward poetry—or their appreciation of it—has changed.

2. There are eight poems in this unit. Work with three other students to read all of them aloud. Each group member should choose two poems to practice and present to the rest of the class. Begin by reading the poems aloud to each other. After each member reads his or her poems aloud once, ask everyone to suggest ways to improve the presentation. For example, suggestions can be about timing, about which words to emphasize in particular poems, and about how to pronounce difficult words. Allow time for each group member to practice his or her readings and then present your readings to the rest of the class.

3. There are many ways to categorize poems. Work with a small group to group the poems in this unit into poems about nature and poems about people. Then take a second look at all the poems and group them as rhyming or not rhyming. Finally, group the poems as humorous and lighthearted or serious. Keep track of the poems that fit into each category and read your lists to the class. See if every group listed the same poems in the same categories.

WRITE A SELF-PORTRAIT IN VERSE

In this unit you have looked at some of the general characteristics of a poem. In the writing exercises you have practiced applying some of those characteristics. Now you will use what you have learned to write a self-portrait in the form of a poem.

Follow these steps to write your poem. If you have questions about the writing process, refer to Using the Writing Process on page 245.

- Assemble and review the work you did for all the writing exercises in this unit: 1) three lists of personal qualities or characteristics, 2) two short poems—one in traditional form and one in nontraditional form—about qualities or characteristics from your lists, 3) two or more sentences listing sensory details about you, 4) three comparisons relating you and nonhuman things.
- Decide whether you will use a traditional or nontraditional form of poetry for your self-portrait. Then decide on an approximate length. Your poem should be at least eight lines long.
- Choose the qualities or characteristics you would like to discuss in your poem. Then write your poem. Make sure you use at least one comparison that expresses one of the qualities or characteristics. It can be one that you wrote for an earlier exercise, or it can be a new one.
- Proofread your poem for spelling and grammar errors. If your punctuation and capitalization are nonstandard, have a reason for what you use. Make a final copy of your poem. Then share it with a classmate who knows you well and invite his or her response.
- Keep a copy of your poem in your writing portfolio.

Speakers in Poetry

The Corn
by Daniel David Moses

To Julia de Burgos
by Julia de Burgos,
translated by Maria Arrillaga

I Heard a Fly Buzz
by Emily Dickinson

Two Friends
by David Ignatow

Girls Can We Educate We Dads?
by James Berry

Rice and Rose Bowl Blues
by Diane Mei Lin Mark

My Last Duchess
by Robert Browning

Flannan Isle
by Wilfrid Wilson Gibson

**The Deacon's Masterpiece; or,
The Wonderful "One-Hoss Shay"**
by Oliver Wendell Holmes

INTRODUCTION

ABOUT THE LESSONS

Poets are not satisfied with being only themselves. They often imagine what it would be like to be someone else—or even some*thing* else. Mentally, they place themselves into the minds of different characters and speak from their points of view. For example, they might imagine the thoughts of a long distance runner or an ant carrying a bread crumb back to the anthill or a hockey puck about to be hit. When poets write, they assume the identities of anyone or anything that they can imagine. The person or thing whose thoughts they record is called the *speaker* of the poem.

In this unit you will explore the role of the speaker in nine poems. The poems are divided into three groups. The poems in Group 1 provide examples of the various kinds of speakers you are likely to encounter in poems. The poems in Group 2 feature speakers engaged in *monologues*—poems with only one speaker—and *dialogues*—poems with more than one speaker. The poems in Group 3 provide examples of the roles of speakers in narrative poems.

WRITING: DEVELOPING A MONOLOGUE

In the writing exercises in this unit you will develop a poem in which a single speaker talks in a one-sided conversation. At this time, begin your poem by following these steps:

- Think of characters from history whom you find interesting and want to know more about. Your characters may be well-known historical figures, such as Julius Caesar, or unknown people who participated in a movement, such as an anonymous woman who was traveling with a wagon train on the Oregon Trail.
- For each character you list, think of a subject that he or she might have strong opinions about and record it next to his or her name.
- Save your notes to use in later writing exercises.

ABOUT THIS POET

Oliver Wendell Holmes (1809–1894) was born in Cambridge, Massachusetts. He was a physician as well as a poet and an essayist. He received his M.D. degree from Harvard and later taught at and served as dean of its medical school. His engaging and entertaining style of speaking made his classes quite popular at Harvard.

While still a medical student, Holmes wrote his famous poem "Old Ironsides." This poem is credited with saving the warship *Constitution* from being destroyed. Holmes wrote essays and poems throughout his careers as professor and physician. He first gained national attention with his series of essays that appeared in the first few issues of *Atlantic Monthly*, a magazine that he and several other writers founded. His witty columns from that magazine were eventually published in a popular book, *The Autocrat of the Breakfast-Table* (1858), in which Holmes, speaking as a resident of a fictional boarding house, shared his opinions about human nature, science, and religion. This elegant, energetic man made use of his considerable speaking skills in public lectures on literature and continued to write poetry, light verse, and essays into his early 80s.

AS YOU READ

As you read each poem in this unit, ask yourself these questions about the speaker:

- Who is the speaker in this poem? How does the choice of speaker affect the poem's message?
- What is the personality of the speaker or speakers in this poem?
- What role does the speaker play in this poem?

The Corn

by Daniel David Moses

ABOUT THE SELECTION

Daniel David Moses (1952–), a Delaware Indian, was born in Ontario, Canada, on Six Nations land. He graduated from York University in Ontario and then earned another degree in creative writing from the University of British Columbia. He published his first collection of poems in 1980. In addition to poetry, Moses has written plays, teleplays, reviews, and short stories. He is quite active in efforts to promote Native American arts. You will soon see that Moses himself is not the speaker in this poem. Who is the speaker?

I'd already lost my hair. Now my sun
fed children have been taken somewhere. Next

I'll lose these comfortable shoes of mud
to the cold—and be unconcerned. After

all, I no longer need a firm foothold.
There's no flood of light anymore—to stand

in and turn toward. Trickling away, the low
sun's only laying shadows out. They don't

move or fulfill one or feed some. Nor do
they do a thing for one's colour.[1] One's left

[1] British spelling of the word *color*

with only crystals of frost growing—no
childish ears to get brightly wet behind,

no hands to wave as you stand whispering
about the land. Those children were taken

as I said and my hands grew as heavy
as ice, caressing only emptiness.

They dropped off and soon I'd guess the rest of
me will be ready to follow. Down through

the icebound soil to underground fields where
stars are planted in hills. At least that's what

I've seen, staring through the frost. Light will not
be lost but will grow and bud green again.

To Julia de Burgos

by Julia de Burgos, translated by Maria Arrillaga

ABOUT THE SELECTION

Julia de Burgos was born around 1914 in Carolina, Puerto Rico. She was the oldest of 13 children, and her father was a farmer. Because her family was not wealthy, neighbors made donations to support her education. After graduation, de Burgos taught for a short time at the University of Havana in Cuba. She published her first book of poetry in 1938. After she came to the United States in 1940 she suffered from ill health. She died in 1953 virtually penniless and unknown, away from her native land. In 1961, eight years after her death, her work was rediscovered and published in a single volume called *Collected Works.* The poem presented here has also been published in Spanish; this version is a translation.

The word is out that I am your enemy
that in my poetry I am giving you away.

They lie, Julia de Burgos. They lie, Julia de Burgos.
That voice that rises in my poems is not yours: it is my voice;
you are the covering and I the essence;
and between us lies the deepest chasm.

You are the frigid doll of social falsehood,
and I, the virile[1] sparkle of human truth.

You are honey of courtly hypocrisy, not I;
I bare my heart in all my poems.

---

[1] forceful; vigorous

You are selfish, like your world, not I;
I gamble everything to be what I am.

You are but the grave lady, ladylike;
not I; I am life, and strength, and I am woman.

You belong to your husband, your master, not I;
I belong to no one or to everyone, because to all, to all
I give myself in pure feelings and in my thoughts.

You curl your hair, and paint your face, not I;
I am curled by the wind, painted by the sun.

You are lady of the house, resigned and meek,
tied to the prejudices of men, not I;
smelling the horizons of the justice of God.
I am Rocinante,[2] running headlong.

---

[2] the horse of Don Quixote, a fictional character who was known for his idealism and reckless courage

I Heard a Fly Buzz

by Emily Dickinson

ABOUT THE SELECTION

Emily Dickinson (1830–1886) was born in Amherst, Massachusetts, and lived most of her life on the second floor of her family home there. She was a solitary, reclusive woman who always wore white and rarely left her rooms. Although only a few of her approximately 1,800 poems were published during her lifetime, years after her death she has been recognized as one of America's finest poets. In this poem, as in most of her work, she looks at the world from a slightly alternative point of view.

I heard a Fly buzz—when I died—
The Stillness in the Room
Was like the Stillness in the Air—
Between the Heaves of Storm—

The Eyes around—had wrung them dry—
And Breaths were gathering firm
For that last Onset—when the King
Be witnessed—in the Room—

I willed my Keepsakes—Signed away
What portion of me be
Assignable—and then it was
There interposed a Fly—

With Blue—uncertain stumbling Buzz—
Between the light—and me—
And then the Windows failed—and then
I could not see to see—

Two Friends

by David Ignatow

ABOUT THE SELECTION

David Ignatow (1914–1997) was born in Brooklyn, New York. His mother immigrated to the United States from Austria-Hungary, and his father was born in Ukraine. Ignatow worked as a research writer, an office manager at a book bindery, a Western Union auto messenger, an admitting clerk at a hospital, and a paper salesman. In 1948 he started his literary career by publishing his first book of poetry. Soon he became editor of the *Beloit Poetry Journal,* a position he held for nine years. Ignatow wrote numerous books of poetry and lectured about poetry at many American universities. Over the years he received several honors, including an award from the National Institute of Arts and Letters and the Bollingen Prize. What kind of relationship do you think the two friends in this poem have?

I have something to tell you.
I'm listening.
I'm dying.
I'm sorry to hear.
I'm growing old.
It's terrible.
It is, I thought you should know.
Of course and I'm sorry. Keep in touch.
I will and you too.
And let me know what's new.
Certainly, though it can't be much.
And stay well.
And you too.
And go slow.
And you too.

Girls Can We Educate We Dads?

by James Berry

ABOUT THE SELECTION

James Berry (1924 –   ) was born in Jamaica and has lived most of his life in England and Jamaica. Berry was first recognized for his poetry in the National Poetry Competition of Great Britain in 1981. Since then he has written short stories, children's books, and poetry. His work often reflects his Caribbean heritage. He chooses to write in the dialect of his home because, as he says, "life has given us a rich variety of language. And if we celebrate one language over the many, we are deprived. When people share, they are joyful and enriched." How do you think Berry's use of dialect adds to the enjoyment of the following poem?

Listn the male chauvinist in mi dad—
a girl walkin night street mus be bad.
He dohn sey, the world's a free place
for a girl to keep her unmolested space.
Instead he sey—a girl is a girl.

He sey a girl walkin swingin hips about
call boys to look and shout.
He dohn sey, if a girl have style
she wahn to sey, look
I okay from top to foot.
Instead he sey—a girl is a girl.

Listn the male chauvinist in mi dad—
a girl too laughy-laughy look too glad-glad
jus like a girl too looky-looky roun
will get a pretty satan at her side.
He dohn sey—a girl full of go
dohn wahn stifle talent comin on show.
Instead he sey—a girl is a girl.

Rice and Rose Bowl Blues

by Diane Mei Lin Mark

ABOUT THE SELECTION

Diane Mei Lin Mark is both a poet and a filmmaker. She was co-producer of a film called *Picture Bride,* which was shown at the prestigious Sundance Film Festival in 1994. The influence of her Asian-American upbringing is unmistakable in the words of this poem's speaker.

I remember the day
Mama called me in from
the football game with brothers
and neighbor boys
in our front yard

said it was time
I learned to
wash rice for dinner

glancing out the window
I watched a pass interception
setting the other team up
on our 20
    Pour some water
    into the pot,
    she said pleasantly,
    turning on the tap
    Rub the rice
    between your hands,
    pour out the clouds,
    fill it again
    (I secretly traced
    an end run through
    the grains in
    between pourings)

with the rice
settled into a simmer
I started out the door
but was called back

the next day
Roland from across the street
sneeringly said he heard
I couldn't play football
anymore

I laughed loudly,
asking him
where
he'd heard
such a thing

My Last Duchess

by Robert Browning

ABOUT THE SELECTION

Robert Browning (1812–1889) was one of the most critically acclaimed poets of the Victorian Age in England, but he was not recognized as a great poet until late in his life. Browning's work is known for its vigor, optimism, and faith in humanity. In 1846 he married Elizabeth Barrett, also a poet, and they moved to Florence, Italy, where Elizabeth died in 1861. When Browning returned to England, his poetry was so well-received that when he died he was buried with honor in Westminster Abbey, a London church in which many kings, queens, and other famous people are buried.

The speakers in Browning's poems are often historic characters. In this particular poem, the speaker is a duke whose first wife died suddenly after the duke decided she was too free with her smiles. Now the duke wants to marry again, this time choosing the daughter of a count. Before negotiating with the count's assistant, he points out pieces of art in his palace.

That's my last Duchess painted on the wall,
Looking as if she were alive. I call
That piece a wonder, now: Frà Pandolf's[1] hands
Worked busily a day, and there she stands.
Will't please you sit and look at her? I said
"Frà Pandolf" by design, for never read
Strangers like you that pictured countenance,[2]

---

[1] a particular artist

[2] face

The depth and passion of its earnest glance,
But to myself they turned (since none puts by
The curtain I have drawn for you, but I)
And seemed as they would ask me, if they durst,[3]
How such a glance came there; so, not the first
Are you to turn and ask thus. Sir, 't was not
Her husband's presence only, called that spot
Of joy into the Duchess' cheek: perhaps
Frà Pandolf chanced to say "Her mantle laps
Over my lady's wrist too much," or "Paint
Must never hope to reproduce the faint
Half-flush that dies along her throat": such stuff
Was courtesy, she thought, and cause enough
For calling up that spot of joy. She had
A heart—how shall I say?—too soon made glad,
Too easily impressed; she liked whate'er
She looked on, and her looks went everywhere.
Sir, 't was all one! My favor at her breast,
The dropping of the daylight in the West,
The bough of cherries some officious[4] fool
Broke in the orchard for her, the white mule
She rode with round the terrace—all and each
Would draw from her alike the approving speech,
Or blush, at least. She thanked men,—good! but thanked
Somehow—I know not how—as if she ranked
My gift of a nine-hundred-years-old name
With anybody's gift. Who'd stoop to blame
This sort of trifling? Even had you skill
In speech—(which I have not)—to make your will
Quite clear to such an one, and say, "Just this
Or that in you disgusts me; here you miss,
Or there exceed the mark"—and if she let
Herself be lessoned so, nor plainly set
Her wits to yours, forsooth, and made excuse,

---

[3] dare

[4] forward in offering help or advice

—E'en then would be some stooping; and I choose
Never to stoop. Oh sir, she smiled, no doubt,
Whene'er I passed her; but who passed without
Much the same smile? This grew; I gave commands;
Then all smiles stopped together. There she stands
As if alive. Will't please you rise? We'll meet
The company below, then. I repeat,
The Count your master's known munificence[5]
Is ample warrant that no just pretense[6]
Of mine for dowry will be disallowed;[7]
Though his fair daughter's self, as I avowed
At starting, is my object. Nay, we'll go
Together down, sir. Notice Neptune, though,
Taming a sea horse, thought a rarity,
Which Claus of Innsbruck cast in bronze for me!

[5] generosity

[6] claim

[7] refused; rejected as improper

Flannan Isle

by Wilfrid Wilson Gibson

ABOUT THE SELECTION

W. W. Gibson (1878–1962) was an English poet. At first, he wrote long narrative poems about fantastic subjects such as King Arthur's court, but later he focused on the problems and experiences of common people. He based the following poem upon an actual mystery: On December 26, 1900, a supply ship landed on Flannan Isle in the Outer Hebrides, islands in the Atlantic Ocean west of Scotland. The crew members were puzzled because the usually faithful light in the lighthouse was out. When they searched the small lighthouse, they couldn't find any of the three lighthouse keepers. Everything was in perfect order—only the keepers had vanished.

"Though three men dwell on Flannan Isle
To keep the lamp alight,
As we steered under the lee, we caught
No glimmer through the night!"

A passing ship at dawn had brought
The news; and quickly we set sail,
To find out what strange thing might ail
The keepers of the deep-sea light.
The winter day broke blue and bright,
With glancing sun and glancing spray,
While o'er the swell our boat made way,
As gallant as a gull in flight.

But as we neared the lonely Isle,
And looked up at the naked height,
And saw the lighthouse towering white,
With blinded lantern that all night
Had never shot a spark
Of comfort through the dark,
So ghostly in the cold sunlight
It seemed that we were struck the while
With wonder all too dread for words.

And as into the tiny creek
We stole beneath the hanging crag,
We saw three queer, black, ugly birds—
Too big by far in my belief
For guillemot or shag[1]—
Like seamen sitting bolt upright
Upon a half-tide reef;
But as we neared, they plunged from sight
Without a sound or spurt of white.
And still too mazed[2] to speak,

We landed, and made fast the boat,
And climbed the track in single file—
Each wishing he were safe afloat
On any sea, however far,
So be it far from Flannan Isle:
And still we seemed to climb and climb,
As though we'd lost all count of time,
And so must climb forevermore.
Yet all too soon we reached the door—
The black, sun-blistered lighthouse door,
That gaped for us ajar.

---

[1] kinds of sea birds

[2] amazed

As on the threshold for a spell
We paused, we seemed to breathe the smell
Of limewash and of tar,
Familiar as our daily breath,
As though 'twere some strange scent of death:
And so, yet wondering, side by side
We stood a moment, still tongue-tied:
And each with black foreboding eyed
The door, ere we should fling it wide
To leave the sunlight for the gloom:
Till, plucking courage up, at last
Hard on each other's heels we passed
Into the living room.

Yet as we crowded through the door,
We only saw a table, spread
For dinner, meat and cheese and bread;
But all untouched; and no one there;
As though when they sat down to eat,
Ere they could even taste,
Alarm had come; and they in haste
Had risen and left the bread and meat:
For at the table-head a chair
Lay tumbled on the floor.
We listened; but we only heard
The feeble chirping of a bird
That starved upon its perch:
And, listening still, without a word
We set about our hopeless search.

We hunted high, we hunted low;
And soon ransacked the empty house;
Then o'er the island, to and fro,
We ranged, to listen and to look
In every cranny, cleft, or nook
That might have hid a bird or mouse.
But though we searched from shore to shore,

We found no sign in any place:
And soon again stood face to face
Before the gaping door:
And stole into the room once more
As frightened children steal.

Ay: though we hunted high and low,
And hunted everywhere,
Of the three men's fate we found no trace
Of any kind in any place,
But a door ajar, and an untouched meal,
And an overtoppled chair.

And so we listened in the gloom
Of that forsaken living room—
A chill clutch on our breath—
We thought how ill-chance came to all
Who kept the Flannan Light;
And how the rock had been the death
Of many a likely lad;
How six had come to a sudden end,
And three had gone stark mad:

And one whom we'd all known as friend
Had leapt from the lantern one still night,
And fallen dead by the lighthouse wall:
And long we thought
On the three we sought,
And of what might yet befall.

Like curs a glance has brought to heel,
We listened, flinching there:
And looked, and looked, on the untouched meal
And the overtoppled chair.

We seemed to stand for an endless while,
Though still no word was said,
Three men alive on Flannan Isle,
Who thought on three men dead.

The Deacon's Masterpiece; or, The Wonderful "One-Hoss Shay"
A Logical Story

by Oliver Wendell Holmes

ABOUT THE SELECTION

Oliver Wendell Holmes (1809–1894), born in Cambridge, Massachusetts, was a physician as well as a poet and an essayist. He received his M.D. degree from Harvard and later taught at and served as dean of its medical school. For more about Holmes, see About This Poet at the beginning of this unit. As you read this poem, try to imagine Holmes himself as the narrator who is telling the story of an unusual shay, or carriage.

Have you heard of the wonderful one-hoss shay,
That was built in such a logical way
It ran a hundred years to a day,
And then, of a sudden, it—ah, but stay,
I'll tell you what happened without delay,
Scaring the parson into fits,
Frightening people out of their wits,—
Have you heard of that, I say?

SEVENTEEN HUNDRED AND FIFTY-FIVE.
Georgius Secundus[1] was then alive,—
Snuffy old drone from the German hive.
That was the year when Lisbon-town
Saw the earth open and gulp her down,
And Braddock's army was done so brown,
Left without a scalp to its crown.
It was on the terrible, Earthquake-day
That the Deacon finished the one-hoss shay.

---

[1] King George II of England

Now in building of chaises,[2] I tell you what,
There is always *somewhere* a weakest spot,—
In hub, tire, felloe,[3] in spring or thill,[4]
In panel, or crossbar, or floor, or sill,
In screw, bolt, thoroughbrace,—lurking still,
Find it somewhere you must and will,—
Above or below, or within or without,—
And that's the reason, beyond a doubt,
A chaise *breaks down*, but doesn't *wear out*.

But the Deacon swore (as Deacons do,
With an "I dew vum," or an "I tell *yeou*")
He would build one shay to beat the taown
'N the keounty 'n' all the kentry raoun':
It should be so built that it *couldn'* break daown:
"Fur," said the Deacon, " 't's mighty plain
Thut the weakes' places mus' stan' the strain;
'N' the way t' fix it, uz I maintain, is only jest
T' make that place uz strong uz the rest."

So the Deacon inquired of the village folk
Where he could find the strongest oak,
That couldn't be split nor bent nor broke,—
That was for spokes and floor and sills;
He sent for lancewood to make the thills;
The crossbars were ash, from the straightest trees;
The panels of whitewood, that cuts like cheese,
But lasts like iron for things like these;
The hubs of logs from the "Settler's ellum,"—
Last of its timber, —they couldn't sell 'em,
Never an axe had seen their chips,
And the wedges flew from between their lips,
Their blunt ends frizzled like celery-tips;
Step and prop-iron, bolt and screw,

---

[2] carriages

[3] exterior rim of a wheel supported by spokes

[4] shaft of a vehicle

Spring, tire, axle, and linchpin too,
Steel of the finest, bright and blue;
Thoroughbrace bison-skin, thick and wide;
Boot, top, dasher, from tough old hide
Found in the pit when the tanner died.
That was the way he "put her through."
"There!" said the Deacon, "naow she'll dew!"

Do! I tell you, I rather guess
She was a wonder, and nothing less!
Colts grew horses, beards turned gray,
Deacon and deaconess dropped away,
Children and grandchildren—where were they?
But there stood the stout old one-hoss shay
As fresh as on Lisbon-earthquake-day!

EIGHTEEN HUNDRED;—it came and found
The Deacon's masterpiece strong and sound.
Eighteen hundred increased by ten;—
"Hahnsum kerridge" they called it then.
Eighteen hundred and twenty came;—
Running as usual; much, the same.
Thirty and forty at last arrive,
And then come fifty, and FIFTY-FIVE.
Little of all we value here
Wakes on the morn of its hundredth year
Without both feeling and looking queer.
In fact, there's nothing that keeps its youth,
So far as I know, but a tree and truth.
(This is a moral that runs at large;
Take it.—You're welcome.—No extra charge.)

FIRST OF NOVEMBER,—the Earthquake-day.—
There are traces of age in the one-hoss shay,
A general flavor of mild decay,
But nothing local as one may say.
There couldn't be,—for the Deacon's art
Had made it so like in every part

That there wasn't a chance for one to start,
For the wheels were just as strong as the thills,
And the floor was just as strong as the sills,
And the panels just as strong as the floor,
And the whipple-tree neither less nor more,
And the back-crossbar as strong as the fore,
And spring and axle and hub *encore*.
And yet, *as a whole*, it is past a doubt
In another hour it will be *worn out!*

FIRST OF NOVEMBER, 'Fifty-five!
This morning the parson takes a drive.
Now, small boys, get out of the way!
Here comes the wonderful one-hoss shay,
Drawn by a rat-tailed, ewe-necked bay.
"Huddup!" said the parson. Off went they.
The parson was working his Sunday's text,—
Had got to *fifthly*, and stopped perplexed
At what the—Moses—was coming next.
All at once the horse stood still,
Close by the meet'n'-house on the hill.
—First a shiver, and then a thrill,
Then something decidedly like a spill,—
And the parson was sitting upon a rock,
At half-past nine by the meet'n'-house clock,
Just the hour of the Earthquake shock!
—What do you think the parson found,
When he got up and stared around?
The poor old chaise in a heap or mound,
As if it had been to the mill and ground!
You see, of course, if you're not a dunce,
How it went to pieces all at once,—
All at once, and nothing first,—
Just as bubbles do when they burst.

End of the wonderful one-hoss shay.
Logic is logic. That's all I say.

UNDERSTANDING THE POEMS

Record your answers to these questions in your personal literature notebook. Follow the directions for each group.

GROUP 1

Reread the poems in Group 1 to complete these sentences.

Reviewing the Selection

1. The season the speaker is describing in "The Corn" is
   a. late fall.
   b. late summer.
   c. early summer.
   d. spring.

2. Before the speaker in "I Heard a Fly Buzz" notices the fly, he or she
   a. sees a King enter the room.
   b. signs away his or her keepsakes.
   c. starts to cry.
   d. opens the window.

Interpreting the Selection

3. In "To Julia de Burgos" the speaker's feelings toward Julia are
   a. admiring.
   b. contemptuous.
   c. worried.
   d. indifferent.

Recognizing How Words Are Used

4. When the speaker in "The Corn" refers to its "sun-fed children," it is talking about its
   a. caretakers.
   b. roots.
   c. ripe ears of corn.
   d. leaves.

Appreciating Poetry

5. When the speaker in "I Heard a Fly Buzz" compares the stillness in the room to the "the Stillness . . ./Between the Heaves of Storm," he or she suggests a feeling of
   a. absolute joy.
   b. despair that life is coming to a close.
   c. peace and calm.
   d. expectation for what is coming next.

GROUP 2

Reread the poems in Group 2 to complete these sentences.

Reviewing the Selection

6. Before Mama calls the speaker in "Rice and Rose Bowl Blues" to come inside, the speaker has been
   a. having an argument with her brothers.
   b. talking with her friend Roland.
   c. playing football with brothers and neighbors.
   d. watching a football game on television.

7. In "Two Friends" the first speaker tells the second speaker that he or she is
   a. dying.
   b. going on vacation.
   c. depressed.
   d. making plans for the future.

Interpreting the Selection

8. Because the duke's wife in "My Last Duchess" is easily pleased by any small courtesy, the duke feels
   a. nervous that she will leave him for someone else who treats her better.
   b. more loving and tender toward her because he appreciates her simplicity.
   c. disappointed, hurt, and unsure of his worth to her.
   d. angry with her inability to tell gifts of great value from those of little worth.

Recognizing How Words Are Used

9. In "Girls Can We Educate We Dads?" the poet spells the word *listen* as *listn* in order to
   a. show that the speaker doesn't know how to spell.
   b. imitate the sound of the speaker's way of talking.
   c. prove that certain words can be spelled in a number of ways.
   d. make fun of the speaker's way of talking.

Appreciating Poetry

10. The mood of "My Last Duchess" can be described as
   a. angry.
   b. mysterious.
   c. humorous.
   d. menacing.

GROUP 3

Reread the poems in Group 3 to complete these sentences.

Reviewing the Selection

11. The searchers in "Flannan Isle" find all of the following *except*
   a. one chair that had fallen over.
   b. a table set for a meal.
   c. the lighthouse's light still operating on its own.
   d. three black birds.

12. Other lighthouse keepers had also met misfortunes, including
   a. losing all their money.
   b. becoming lost at sea.
   c. killing one another.
   d. going stark mad.

Interpreting the Selection

13. In "The Deacon's Masterpiece" the most amazing difference between the one-hoss shay and other vehicles is that it
   a. scares people as it is driven past them.
   b. needs only one horse to work properly.
   c. lasts for 100 years and falls apart all at once.
   d. was made with care by a deacon.

Recognizing How Words Are Used

14. In “The Deacon’s Masterpiece” the lines “That was the year when Lisbon-town/Saw the earth open and gulp her down” refer to
   a. *Georgius Secundus.*
   b. an earthquake in a city in Portugal.
   c. the earth.
   d. an unnamed woman in Lisbon.

Appreciating Poetry

15. In “The Deacon’s Masterpiece” the speaker’s attitude toward the audience is one of
   a. contempt.
   b. formality and properness.
   c. respect.
   d. friendliness and good humor.

Now check your answers with your teacher. Study the questions you answered incorrectly. What types of questions were they? Talk with your teacher about ways to work on those skills.

Speakers in Poetry

The speaker is the person or thing whose words and thoughts you read in a poem. It cannot be assumed that the speaker is the poet because poets often assume different identities for every poem they write. Sometimes they "try on" new personalities to explore what a particular person or thing might be thinking about or feeling.

Whether a poem's speaker is telling his or her own thoughts or is describing someone or something as an observer, the speaker's voice affects the entire poem. Many poetic elements, including mood, theme and meaning, are intertwined with the speaker's personality, style, and attitude. For that reason, to understand a poem well, it is essential to understand the poem's speaker well.

The lessons in this unit focus on the speakers in selected poems. All of the poems have strong, distinct speakers who enable the poet to convey his or her message. The lessons will discuss these ideas:

1. To convey ideas or feelings most effectively, a poet may use a *persona,* or personality, and a voice other than his or her own.
2. You can learn about a poem's speaker through his or her choice of subject and style of speaking.
3. In some poems the speaker is the narrator of a story. The narrator's voice helps establish the poem's mood and tone.

LESSON 1

THE ROLE OF THE SPEAKER

Most poets feel their own emotions deeply and are aware of the feelings of those around them. When they speak in their poetry, they may choose to give voice to their own emotions and thoughts, or they may speak as another person or even an object whose thoughts and feelings they can only imagine. When they speak using a new personality, we say they are using a different persona. *Persona* is a Latin word meaning "mask."

The persona is the mask that the poet hides behind in order to get across his or her ideas most effectively. For example, a poet may speak as a survivor of a concentration camp to emphasize the importance of peace and love. A poet may speak as an extinct dodo bird to encourage readers to take care of endangered species. A poet may speak as the wind to focus on the power of nature.

In Emily Dickinson's "I Heard a Fly Buzz" the speaker talks to us from beyond the grave. Dickinson could have addressed the subject of death in any number of ways, speaking as herself. When she speaks through the persona of a deceased person, however, she grabs your attention from the very first line:

> I heard a Fly buzz—when I died—
> The Stillness in the Room
> Was like the Stillness in the Air—
> Between the Heaves of Storm—

When you read the poem for the first time, you probably couldn't help but be surprised and a little confused. If the speaker has died, how can he or she be writing about death experiences? And why is he or she concentrating on an inconsequential detail such as a fly in the midst of this unfortunate passage? The matter-of-fact tone that the speaker uses takes the sorrow out of the experience and replaces it with an objective indifference.

In "To Julia de Burgos" the poet imagines a separate personality living inside herself. She allows that persona to speak in the poem:

> The word is out that I am your enemy
> that in my poetry I am giving you away.
>
> They lie, Julia de Burgos. They lie, Julia de Burgos.
> That voice that rises in my poems is not yours: it is my voice;
> you are the covering and I the essence;
> and between us lies the deepest chasm.

The speaker feels contempt for the person that Julia allows society to see, calling Julia the "frigid doll of social falsehood" and herself the "virile sparkle of human truth." By speaking in the voice of the inner Julia, the poet conveys the idea that she often feels split into two personalities—the one who lives by society's rules and the one who thinks and feels entirely independent of them.

EXERCISE 1

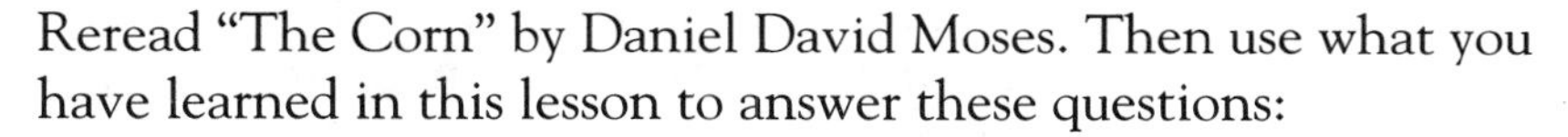

Reread "The Corn" by Daniel David Moses. Then use what you have learned in this lesson to answer these questions:

1. Who is the speaker in this poem? At what point in the poem did you realize the speaker's identity?
2. Why do you think the poet has chosen this speaker? What are some advantages of speaking from this point of view?

Now check your answers with your teacher. Review this part of the lesson if you don't understand why an answer was incorrect.

WRITING ON YOUR OWN 

In the previous writing exercise you listed possible historical figures that you could use in a poem. Now follow these steps:

- Look over the list of possible historical figures that you prepared earlier in the unit. Choose one person to be the speaker of your poem.
- Do some research on your chosen historical figure and take notes on his or her life. If the person is not famous, take notes on what people were like during your chosen time period or event. You can use your notes to create a *composite character*, a combination of several different people.

- Use your notes to write a short paragraph explaining who your speaker will be and why you decided on him or her; that is, what about that person's life—or that particular time period or event—particularly interests you?
- Save your notes in your writing portfolio.

LESSON 2 LEARNING ABOUT THE SPEAKER

In many poems the speaker talks directly to the reader. In a kind of one-sided conversation, the speaker shares a thought or an emotion, relates a story, or tries to persuade the reader to think a certain way. As you learned earlier in this unit, poems in which only one character speaks are referred to as monologues.

Through monologues, readers learn much about the speaker. Look, for example, at "Girls Can We Educate We Dads?" by James Berry. The speaker is talking to you, the reader, sharing her frustration and outrage at her father's rigid and unsympathetic attitude toward women:

> Listn the male chauvinist in mi dad—
> a girl walkin night street mus be bad.
> He dohn sey, the world's a free place
> for a girl to keep her unmolested space.
> Instead he sey—a girl is a girl.

The first time you read this poem, you probably were immediately struck by the speaker's use of *dialect*, or way of speaking that is characteristic of a particular group of people. The speaker's dialect alerted you to the fact that she is from the West Indies, probably Jamaica, where Berry lived for many years. But then your attention probably returned to the content of the speaker's words. She is angry. She feels that her father's rules for girls don't allow her to be a whole person, free to talk, walk, and dress as she wishes. She wants to reveal her father's unreasonableness: "Instead he sey—a girl is a girl." Clearly, the speaker is a young woman who is full of energy and self-confidence and who will not be happy in the role that her father has chosen for girls.

"My Last Duchess" by Robert Browning features a slightly different kind of monologue called a dramatic monologue. A *dramatic monologue* is a poem with a single speaker engaged in a dramatic situation. The speaker is a character involved in an actual or imagined story. Although the poem may not tell the entire story, it does reveal the speaker's thoughts. For example, in "My Last Duchess" the speaker is a selfish and evil duke showing a count's representative some of his treasured art works, including a painting of his dead wife. The duke's pride and lack of compassion come through clearly in his references to the wife he had killed:

> —E'en then would be some stooping; and I choose
> Never to stoop. Oh sir, she smiled, no doubt,
> Whene'er I passed her; but who passed without
> Much the same smile? This grew; I gave commands;
> Then all smiles stopped together. There she stands
> As if alive. . . .

The duke chose not to stoop to reasoning or arguing with his wife. It was beneath him to try to convince her that his gifts were of more value than anyone else's attentions to her. So, without remorse or guilt, he admits that he "gave commands" to make sure that her pointless and frivolous smiles "stopped altogether." He seems proud of his own decisiveness and good sense as he shows the painting and tells the story. Through his words, the speaker paints a heartless picture of himself and if the count's representative has any decency, he will recommend that the count find another match for his daughter.

"Two Friends" by David Ignatow features not one, but two speakers. It is an example of a *dialogue*, a conversation between two (or more) characters. Because there is no traditional indication that a new character is speaking, you need to pay particular attention as you read. The two speakers trade lines throughout the poem, with the first speaker's words alternating with the second speaker's. What do you learn about these speakers through their words—both what they are saying and how they say it?

> I have something to tell you.
> I'm listening.
> I'm dying.
> I'm sorry to hear.
> I'm growing old.
> It's terrible.
> It is, I thought you should know.
> Of course and I'm sorry. Keep in touch.

The first speaker casually drops a virtual bombshell—"I'm dying." The second speaker responds with an almost unbelievably callous "I'm sorry to hear," a response whose apathy does not match the importance of the news. After hearing the first speaker's complaint about growing old, the second speaker effectively stops the conversation by telling the first to keep in touch. Although we cannot hear the voices, we can imagine the antiseptic, passionless tones of both participants. Neither speaker puts forth much emotion or true sense of caring for the other. Yet, ironically, the title of the poem is "Two Friends." Can we in all honesty call these two characters friends?

EXERCISE 2

Reread "Rice and Rose Bowl Blues." Then use what you have learned in this lesson to answer these questions:

1. What clues in the poem indicate that the speaker is female? How would you describe the speaker's personality, based on what she remembers about that day? How does the speaker feel about the day's events?
2. Although this poem is a monologue, embedded in it are the words of a second speaker. Identify the second speaker's words. How does the way the poem is printed show that a second speaker is talking?

Now check your answers with your teacher. Review this part of the lesson if you don't understand why an answer was incorrect.

WRITING ON YOUR OWN 

In this lesson you learned that monologues and dialogues reveal much about the speaker or speakers of poems. Now you will use what you learned to decide how to reveal your chosen historical figure's personality. Follow these steps:

- Review what you have learned about your chosen historical figure. Make a list of the most exciting or pivotal parts of his or her life. If you are creating a composite character, list some of the most important events that occurred during your chosen time period or event.
- Choose one event during which you feel that your character's mind would have been filled with strong emotion, perhaps doubt, fear, or joy. Jot down a few notes about emotions and thoughts that he or she might have had at that time.
- Write several sentences that the character might have written in a diary or said to a companion to express his or her thoughts and emotions. Try to make the sentences follow in a logical sequence.

LESSON 3 THE SPEAKER IN NARRATIVE POEMS

You may have had the experience of hearing a hilarious joke told by a stand-up comic or a friend. Later you may have repeated the joke to other friends but didn't get the reaction you had expected from them. They may have laughed or smiled politely when you expected a roar of laughter. If you're like most people, the problem probably was your way of speaking. Somehow in the retelling, you used different words, timing, or emphasis. Maybe your tone of voice was just not as funny as the comic's. Maybe your listeners could not imagine the situation happening to you.

For whatever reason, the joke didn't go over as well as it did when you first heard it from the original speaker. This experience probably taught you that the person who tells a joke or a story often determines the audience's enjoyment of the story.

In both of the poems in Group 3 the speaker, or *narrator*, tells a story. These stories are as different in mood as any two stories can be. In both poems, however, the narrator affects the poem in a number of ways. For example, the narrator of "The Deacon's Masterpiece" sets a light and friendly tone in the first stanza:

> Have you heard of the wonderful one-hoss shay,
> That was built in such a logical way
> It ran a hundred years to a day,
> And then, of a sudden, it—ah, but stay,
> I'll tell you what happened without delay,
> Scaring the parson into fits,
> Frightening people out of their wits,—
> Have you heard of that, I say?

You can just about hear the folksy, casual way in which the speaker is talking, as if you were an old friend. The narrator interrupts the flow of the story, savoring its deliciousness and hoping to prolong the fun. He or she asks you a question: "Have you heard of that, I say?" and prepares you for a humorous tale.

In contrast, "Flannan Isle" begins with a mysterious news report that suggests a potential disaster:

> "Though three men dwell on Flannan Isle
> To keep the lamp alight,
> As we steered under the lee, we caught
> No glimmer through the night!"
>
> A passing ship at dawn had brought
> The news; and quickly we set sail,
> To find out what strange thing might ail
> The keepers of the deep-sea light.

Immediately upon hearing the news that the light is not shining at night, the speaker assumes that a "strange thing might ail/The keepers of the deep-sea light." The narrator shares a sense of disquiet and fear as he or she nears the light. Which words in this excerpt help to increase your own nervousness about the keepers?

> But as we neared the lonely Isle,
> And looked up at the naked height,
> And saw the lighthouse towering white,
> With blinded lantern that all night
> Had never shot a spark
> Of comfort through the dark,
> So ghostly in the cold sunlight
> It seemed that we were struck the while
> With wonder all too dread for words.

The narrator uses words such as *lonely, naked, ghostly, cold, dread*—all words that create a chill in the heart of the reader. The narrator's attitude and presentation prepare you for the strange, unsettling story that is about to unfold. Unlike the narrator of "The Deacon's Masterpiece," this narrator maintains his or her distance from the reader, never talking in a close, intimate way, but simply sharing the eerie story.

EXERCISE 3

Use "The Deacon's Masterpiece" and what you have learned in this lesson to answer these questions:

1. Why do you think the narrator has the Deacon speak in an unusual dialect? What might the narrator be trying to suggest about the character of the Deacon through his use of dialect, as in this passage:

> But the Deacon swore (as Deacons do,
> With an "I dew vum," or an "I tell *yeou*")

2. The narrator specifies all the parts of the shay that the Deacon carefully selected for strength and durability. Most of those parts were probably unfamiliar to you, such as the sills, the thills, the crossbars, the prop-iron, and the dasher. A modern reader doesn't really need to know anything about each of those parts to understand and appreciate the story. Why do you think the narrator mentions them in the description of the building of the shay?

3. Do you think you would like the narrator if you met him or her? Explain why or why not. Do the same for the narrator of "Flannan Isle." Briefly describe and compare their personalities.

Now check your answers with your teacher. Review this part of the lesson if you don't understand why an answer was incorrect.

WRITING ON YOUR OWN

Earlier in the unit you decided on a historical figure for a dramatic monologue. You have researched the person and imagined thoughts that he or she might have had. Now follow these steps:

- Gather the notes that you wrote about your character. Write a brief profile of the person to accompany the poem that you will write at the end of the unit.
- Look over the sentences you wrote for Writing on Your Own 2. Then decide on the mood you would like to convey in your poem. Take into account the personality of your character. For example, if he or she was practical and good-humored, you probably will want the mood of your poem to reflect that.
- Now decide if you want to write a poem that rhymes or not. If you want your poem to rhyme, you may want to use the simple rhyme scheme that Robert Browning uses in "My Last Duchess" or the more complicated rhyme schemes of "Flannan Isle" or "The Deacon's Masterpiece." Then write just the first stanza of the poem. Make sure that the first stanza establishes the mood of the poem and gives readers an idea of the speaker's personality.

DISCUSSION GUIDES

1. With a small group of classmates analyze "Girls Can We Educate We Dads?" line by line. As you read the poem, translate it into the words and dialect that a girl of your locale and time might use, rather than the Jamaican dialect that the poem uses. For example, you might translate "a girl walkin night street" to "a girl who walks down the street at night." If it is more effective, use slang instead of formal, standard English.

2. "Flannan Isle" describes the mysterious disappearance of three lighthouse keepers. This disappearance is not the only mystery that baffles people years afterwards. Discuss various famous mysteries that fascinate the public—for example: the Bermuda Triangle, the disappearance of pilot Amelia Earhart, or the fate of the lost colony of Roanoke. After you list any well-known mysteries, choose one to research. Later, share what you have learned with the rest of the group.

3. "To Julia de Burgos" and the last three poems in Group 2 comment on the role of girls and women in society, both 300 years ago and today. How have women's roles changed through the years? What aspects of their roles have not changed? From what the poems say about being a girl, would you choose to be one? Why or why not? Do you think the poems reflect the truth? Do they tell the whole story about what it means to be a girl or a woman? Which advantages to being a woman have they ignored? Discuss these questions with the class.

4. Oliver Wendell Holmes was said to be an entertaining and engaging public speaker. In all likelihood, he presented "The Deacon's Masterpiece" to many audiences, emphasizing its folksiness and humorously exaggerating the dialect of the Deacon. With at least one other classmate, prepare an oral reading of the poem. Try to make your reading suggest that you are telling the story to a group of friends who have all the time in the world to listen to you. As Holmes did, make your reading as entertaining as possible.

WRITE A DRAMATIC MONOLOGUE

In this unit you have focused on the role of the speaker in poems and have read a variety of poems, including monologues, dialogues, and narrative poems. Now you will write a dramatic monologue in which a single character in a dramatic situation speaks.

Follow these steps to write your dramatic monologue. If you have questions about the writing process, refer to Using the Writing Process on page 245.

- Assemble the work you did for all the writing exercises in this unit: 1) a list of interesting historical figures that could speak in a monologue, 2) a paragraph that identifies your chosen speaker and explains why you chose him or her, 3) several sentences that the speaker might have said to express his or her emotions and thoughts at a crucial time, 4) the brief profile of your historical figure and the first stanza of a dramatic monologue.
- Look over your notes and profile of the person. Do you still want to write about this particular person and event? If not, choose a different person or a different time or event upon which to base your dramatic monologue.
- Make a list of topics that the speaker might want to describe. Any feelings or ideas connected with the crucial event you chose earlier would be appropriate. Then decide who the audience will be. For example, in "My Last Duchess" the duke is speaking to the count's assistant.
- If you have chosen to stick with your original person and event, begin your poem with the stanza that you wrote earlier. If the stanza has a particular rhyme scheme, continue it throughout the poem. Be sure that what the speaker says and the style in which he or she speaks matches his or her personality.

- Read your dramatic monologue aloud and decide if it is consistent with the speaker's personality as you imagine it. Make sure that the mood is clear by having a friend read the poem and describe the mood. If you need to add details or change the style of speech slightly, do so now.
- Proofread your poem for spelling, grammar, and punctuation errors. Then make a final copy and save it in your writing portfolio.

Imagery, Concrete Language, and Mood

Abandoned Farmhouse
by Ted Kooser

The Morning My Father Died, April 7, 1963
by James Masao Mitsui

In an Iridescent Time
by Ruth Stone

I Wandered Lonely As a Cloud
by William Wordsworth

The Proletariat Speaks
by Alice Ruth Moore Dunbar-Nelson

Poem to Be Read at 3 A.M.
by Donald Justice

The Breathing
by Denise Levertov

INTRODUCTION

ABOUT THE LESSONS

No one can stop time. Once a moment passes, it is gone forever. Even so, artists such as writers, painters, and sculptors still try to freeze time, to recall or reproduce a person, place, or event so perfectly that a moment from the past seems to live again. Poets use words to capture particular times when they recreate experiences and events in their poems.

In this unit you will read seven poems that paint word pictures or breathe life into past experiences. These poems are divided into two groups. The poems in Group 1 recreate moments by describing small but significant details that together make unforgettable images. The poems in Group 2 use detailed descriptions of objects and experiences to create particular moods.

WRITING: DESCRIBING A MOMENT

This unit focuses on the techniques that poets use to develop images. At the end of the unit you will write a poem that recreates a particular moment in time. Here are some suggestions to help you start thinking about potential subjects for your poem:

- For one or two days, carry a small notebook around with you. At four widely separated times each day, record what you are experiencing at that moment. Jot down what you are seeing, hearing, smelling, tasting, and touching. Be as specific as possible. For example, don't just record "bad smell"; instead specify "the smell of burnt toast."
- At the same time that you record what your senses are registering at a particular moment, record how you feel and why. Are you feeling rushed? hopeful? peaceful? some other feeling? What is making you feel that way? Record your feelings on the same page as the sensory details for each moment in time.
- Save your notes to use in later writing exercises.

ABOUT THIS POET

William Wordsworth (1770–1850) was one of the founders of the Romantic Movement in English poetry. Early in his writing career he was influenced by a classical, highly structured approach to poetry that was in fashion at the time. Soon, however, Wordsworth rebelled against the rules that had been set up, maintaining that the raw materials of poetry should be sensory experience and emotion. Much of Wordsworth's poetry focuses on nature and the harmony between humans and the natural world. He encouraged readers to rely on intuition and the instincts that all humans are born with, and he believed that humanity gets a glimpse of God through an observation of itself and nature.

At first, Wordsworth's views on poetry were not accepted by literary circles; in fact, they were violently opposed for many years. By 1843, however, critics had changed their minds about the Romantic Movement that Wordsworth had helped to found, and they named him England's poet laureate, or most important poet.

AS YOU READ

As you read each of the poems in this unit, ask yourself these questions:

- To which senses is the poet appealing? Which words are most effective in making the experience seem real?
- How does the poem affect your emotions? What mood do you think the poet is trying to create?

Abandoned Farmhouse

by Ted Kooser

ABOUT THE SELECTION

Ted Kooser (1939–) was born in Iowa and received his bachelor's degree from Iowa State University and his master's degree from the University of Nebraska. For many years, Kooser has written poetry while maintaining a career with an insurance company. Many of his poems reflect his familiarity with the Great Plains area, which is most likely where the following poem is set.

He was a big man, says the size of his shoes
on a pile of broken dishes by the house;
a tall man too, says the length of the bed
in an upstairs room; and a good, God-fearing man,
says the Bible with a broken back
on the floor below the window, dusty with sun;
but not a man for farming, say the fields
cluttered with boulders and the leaky barn.

A woman lived with him, says the bedroom wall
papered with lilacs and the kitchen shelves
covered with oilcloth, and they had a child
says the sandbox made from a tractor tire.
Money was scarce, say the jars of plum preserves
and canned tomatoes sealed in the cellar-hole,
and the winters cold, say the rags in the window frames.
It was lonely here, says the narrow gravel road.

Something went wrong, says the empty house
in the weed-choked yard. Stones in the fields
say he was not a farmer; the still-sealed jars
in the cellar say she left in a nervous haste.
And the child? Its toys are strewn in the yard
like branches after a storm—a rubber cow,
a rusty tractor with a broken plow,
a doll in overalls. Something went wrong, they say.

The Morning My Father Died, April 7, 1963

by James Masao Mitsui

ABOUT THE SELECTION

James Masao Mitsui (1940–) has been both a poet and a high school English teacher. He earned his master's degree at the University of Washington. Mitsui was honored with the Pacific Northwest Booksellers Award for his first book of poetry, *Journal of the Sun.* Notice how he appeals to more than one sense in his description of an emotion-filled morning.

The youngest son, I left the family inside and stood
alone in the unplanted garden by a cherry tree
we had grown ourselves, next to a trash barrel
smoldering what we couldn't give away or move
to Seattle. Looking over the rusty edge I could see
colors of volcano. Feathers of ash floated
up to a sky that was changing. I stared at the sound
of meadowlarks below the water tank
on the pumice-colored hill where the sun would come.
I couldn't stop smelling sagebrush, the creosote[1]
bottoms of posts, the dew that was like a thunderstorm
had passed an hour before. Thoughts were trees
under a lake; that moment was sunflower, killdeer[2]
and cheatgrass. Volunteer wheat grew strong
on the far side of our place along the old highway.
Undeberg's rooster gave the day its sharper edge,
the top of the sun. Turning to go back inside,
twenty years of Big Bend Country
took off like sparrows from a startled fence.

---

[1] poisonous, oily liquid with a very strong odor

[2] North American bird

In an Iridescent[1] Time

by Ruth Stone

ABOUT THE SELECTION

Ruth Stone (1915–), born in Roanoke, Virginia, has published several volumes of poetry and has received a number of poetry awards. She teaches creative writing at the University of New York/Binghamton. Look for the small details that not only paint a picture but also set a mood in this poem.

My mother, when young, scrubbed laundry in a tub,
She and her sisters on an old brick walk
Under the apple trees, sweet rub-a-dub.
The bees came round their heads, the wrens made talk.
Four young ladies each with a rainbow board
Honed their knuckles, wrung their wrists to red,
Tossed back their braids and wiped their aprons wet.
The Jersey calf beyond the back fence roared;
And all the soft day, swarms about their pet
Buzzed at his big brown eyes and bullish head.
Four times they rinsed, they said. Some things they starched,
Then shook them from the baskets two by two,
And pinned the fluttering intimacies of life
Between the lilac bushes and the yew:
Brown gingham, pink, and skirts of Alice blue.[2]

---

[1] rainbow-colored

[2] a light blue, named after the daughter of President Theodore Roosevelt

I Wandered Lonely As a Cloud

by William Wordsworth

ABOUT THE SELECTION

William Wordsworth (1770–1850) was one of the founders of the Romantic Movement in English poetry. Born in England, he was educated at Cambridge University and traveled to France as a young man. He felt a deep appreciation for nature and often based his poetry on natural subjects. For more about Wordsworth, read About This Poet at the beginning of this unit. Wordsworth maintained that poetry came from "emotion recollected in tranquillity," a sentiment that is reflected in the following poem.

I wandered lonely as a cloud
That floats on high o'er vales and hills,
When all at once I saw a crowd,
A host, of golden daffodils;
Beside the lake, beneath the trees,
Fluttering and dancing in the breeze.

Continuous as the stars that shine
And twinkle on the milky way,
They stretched in never-ending line
Along the margin of a bay:
Ten thousand saw I at a glance,
Tossing their heads in sprightly[1] dance.

---

[1] energetic; spirited

The waves beside them danced; but they
Outdid the sparkling waves in glee;
A poet could not but be gay,
In such a jocund[2] company;
I gazed—and gazed—but little thought
What wealth the show to me had brought:

For oft, when on my couch I lie
In vacant or in pensive[3] mood,
They flash upon that inward eye
Which is the bliss of solitude;
And then my heart with pleasure fills,
And dances with the daffodils.

[2] cheerful

[3] thoughtful

The Proletariat[1] Speaks

by Alice Ruth Moore Dunbar-Nelson

ABOUT THE SELECTION

Alice Ruth Moore Dunbar-Nelson (1875–1935) was born in New Orleans and was a teacher for many years. Her poetry brought her into contact with other African American poets who met in Washington, D.C., in a movement reminiscent of the Harlem Renaissance. Although she wrote two collections of short fiction, she never published a full volume of poetry. Her poems are available only in anthologies and periodicals. See if you agree with her sentiments in this poem of opposites.

I love beautiful things:
Great trees, bending green winged branches to a velvet lawn,
Fountains sparkling in white marble basins,
Cool fragrance of lilacs and roses and honeysuckle.
Or exotic blooms, filling the air with heart-contracting odors;
Spacious rooms, cool and gracious with statues and books,
Carven seats and tapestries, and old masters
Whose patina[2] shows the wealth of centuries.

And so I work
In a dusty office, whose grimèd windows
Look out in an alley of unbelievable squalor,[3]
Where mangy cats, in their degradation, spurn
Swarming bits of meat and bread;
Where odors, vile and breathtaking, rise in fetid waves
Filling my nostrils, scorching my humid, bitter cheeks.

---

[1] lowest social class; laboring class that owns no capital

[2] the surface of something that is beautiful because of age or use

[3] filth

I love beautiful things:
Carven tables laid with lily-hued linen
And fragile china and sparkling iridescent glass;
Pale silver, etched with heraldries,[4]
Where tender bits of regal dainties tempt,
And soft-stepped service anticipates the unspoken wish.

And so I eat
In the food-laden air of a greasy kitchen,
At an oil-clothed table:
Plate piled high with food that turns my head away,
Lest a squeamish stomach reject too soon
The lumpy gobs it never needed.
Or in a smoky cafeteria, balancing a slippery tray
To a table crowded with elbows
Which lately the bus boy wiped with a grimy rag.

I love beautiful things:
Soft linen sheets and silken coverlet,
Sweet coolth of chamber opened wide to fragrant breeze;
Rose-shaded lamps and golden atomizers,[5]
Spraying Parisian fragrance over my relaxed limbs,
Fresh from a white marble bath, and sweet cool spray.

And so I sleep
In a hot hall-room whose half opened window,
Unscreened, refuses to budge another inch;
Admits no air, only insects, and hot choking gasps,
That make me writhe,[6] nun-like, in sack-cloth sheets and lumps of straw.

And then I rise
To fight my way to a dubious tub,
Whose tiny, tepid[7] stream threatens to make me late;
And hurrying out, dab my unrefreshed face
With bits of toiletry from the ten cent store.

[4] family insignia, such as coats of arms

[5] tools for spraying fragrances into the air

[6] toss and turn; thrash

[7] lukewarm

Poem to Be Read at 3 A.M.

by Donald Justice

ABOUT THE SELECTION

Donald Justice (1925–) was born in Miami, Florida. He has taught English at the University of Florida at Gainesville and the Iowa Writers Workshop. In 1980 he won the Pulitzer Prize for his volume *Selected Poems*. Notice how he makes us focus on a familiar, seemingly unimportant moment and gives it added meaning.

Excepting the diner
On the outskirts
The town of Ladora
At 3 A.M.
Was dark but
For my headlights
And up in
One second-story room
A single light
Where someone
Was sick or
Perhaps reading
As I drove past
At seventy
Not thinking
This poem
Is for whoever
Had the light on

The Breathing

by Denise Levertov

ABOUT THE SELECTION

Denise Levertov (1923–) was born in England and moved to the United States in 1948. She taught at a number of colleges before retiring from a full professorship at Tufts University. Levertov's topics range from intensely personal to political, taking on issues such as poverty, war, and women's role in society. As you read this poem, imagine the silence of a foggy day.

An absolute[1]
patience.
Trees stand
up to their knees in
fog. The fog
slowly flows
uphill.
          White
cobwebs, the grass
leaning where deer
have looked for apples.
The woods
from brook to where
the top of the hill looks
over the fog, send up
not one bird.
So absolute, it is
no other than
happiness itself, a breathing
too quiet to hear.

---

[1] complete; without limit

UNDERSTANDING THE POEMS

Record your answers to these questions in your personal literature notebook. Follow the directions for each group.

GROUP 1

Reread the poems in Group 1 to complete these items.

Reviewing the Selection

1. The detail in "Abandoned Farmhouse" that suggests that the man who lived there was not a very good farmer is the
   a. pile of broken dishes by the house.
   b. fields cluttered with boulders.
   c. sandbox made from a tractor tire.
   d. jars of preserves left in the cellar-hole.

2. The women in "In an Iridescent Time" are
   a. sweeping a brick walk.
   b. feeding farm animals.
   c. weeding a garden.
   d. washing clothes.

Interpreting the Selection

3. When the speaker in "In an Iridescent Time" says that "the wrens made talk," he or she means that the
   a. wrens were singing and their calls sounded like talking.
   b. women talked about the wrens.
   c. women couldn't hear themselves because the wrens were so loud.
   d. women were talking like singing wrens.

Recognizing How Words Are Used

4. The following phrase from "Abandoned Farmhouse" that does not use alliteration—the repetition of consonant sounds—is
   a. "says the Bible with a broken back."
   b. "says the size of his shoes."
   c. "the still-sealed jars/in the cellar."
   d. "on a pile of broken dishes."

Appreciating Poetry

5. In which of these lines from a poem in Group 1 has the poet combined details about two different senses in the same image?
a. "She and her sisters on an old brick walk/Under the apple trees"
b. "Looking over the rusty edge I could see/colors of a volcano"
c. "I stared at the sound/of meadowlarks"
d. "the bedroom wall/papered with lilacs"

GROUP 2

Reread the poems in Group 2 to complete these sentences.

Reviewing the Selection

6. "Poem to Be Read at 3 A.M." is dedicated to
a. the town of Ladora, which the speaker drove through at 3 A.M.
b. the waitress in the diner on the outskirts of Ladora.
c. whoever had the light on in the window as the speaker drove by.
d. the speaker's spouse.

7. The speaker in "I Wandered Lonely As a Cloud" is particularly delighted when he or she sees
a. clouds floating through the sky.
b. the waves on the ocean.
c. the stars shining in the sky.
d. a great number of golden daffodils.

Interpreting the Selection

8. The speaker in "The Proletariat Speaks" complains that
a. the people in her life are cruel.
b. reality doesn't live up to her dreams.
c. her job doesn't challenge her enough.
d. she has too many beautiful things.

Recognizing How Words Are Used

9. In "The Breathing" the phrases "An absolute" and "So absolute" are an example of
a. alliteration.
b. repetition.
c. rhyme.
d. visual imagery.

Appreciating Poetry

10. The tone, or attitude, of the speaker in "The Proletariat Speaks" can be described as
   a. hopeful.
   b. frustrated.
   c. comical.
   d. practical.

Now check your answers with your teacher. Study the questions you answered incorrectly. What types of questions were they? Talk with your teacher about ways to work on those skills.

Imagery, Concrete Language, and Mood

Some people feel that the major distinguishing feature of poetry is its use of rhyme and rhythm. While it is true that the creative use of these techniques is a major element in poetry, many poems do not rhyme and do not have an obvious rhythm. Instead they rely on *images*, or words that create a mental picture for the reader. Usually images appeal to one or more of the senses—sight, hearing, taste, smell, and touch—and so they are called *sensory images*. One of the most effective ways of creating a sensory image is by using concrete language. *Concrete language* refers to words that describe things that you can experience with your senses. Poets choose just the right images and concrete words to create the ideas and moods they wish to convey.

In the following lessons you will examine poems that use sharp images and concrete language to recreate experiences and set moods. The lessons will discuss these ideas:

1. Poets use sensory details, sensory images, and concrete language to create or recreate particular moments.

2. Every poem has a particular mood. The mood is created through careful choice of specific words and appropriate images.

LESSON 1 SENSORY IMAGES, CONCRETE LANGUAGE, AND EXACT WORDS

If you enter your local convenience store or department store, you are likely to see a video camera operating. The camera's purpose is to record images of all the people who visit the store, just in case a crime occurs and officials need to replay the day's activities. The camera is usually focused on a single spot in the store, such as the doorway or the cash register, and it objectively records images from the same perspective all day long.

If that same video camera were put in the hands of a person, however, the images it would capture would be quite different. When human beings operate cameras, they use their creativity and unique perspectives to subjectively record people and events. For example, instead of filming everything from the exact same distance and perspective as a store camera would, people film scenes from many different angles in order to capture as many unique and interesting details as possible. They also might try to convey a mood or a point of view while filming.

Sometimes poets are like skilled and sensitive camera operators. Using their own unique perspectives and attitudes, they record what they see, hear, smell, taste, and feel. To do this, they use just the right words to create pictures for their readers and to set particular moods.

Some of the techniques that poets use when they want to recreate a moment or an experience are sensory images and concrete language. As mentioned earlier, *sensory images* are pictures painted with words that appeal to one or more senses. *Concrete language* refers to words or phrases that describe something that can be experienced by the senses. For example, *telephone* is a concrete word, while *communication* is not. *English springer spaniel* is an example of concrete language, while *enthusiasm* is not. Concrete language is so specific that it immediately creates an image in the reader's mind and appeals to all the senses that the reader associates with that object. Look for the sensory images and concrete language in this excerpt from "The Morning My Father Died, April 7, 1963" by James Masao Mitsui:

> Looking over the rusty edge I could see
> colors of volcano. Feathers of ash floated
> up to a sky that was changing. I stared at the sound
> of meadowlarks below the water tank
> on the pumice-colored hill where the sun would come.
> I couldn't stop smelling sagebrush, the creosote
> bottoms of posts, the dew that was like a thunderstorm
> had passed an hour before.

You can both see and feel the rusty edge of the trash barrel and the feathers of ash floating through the air. You can see and hear the meadowlark and its song. The sagebrush, the creosote bottoms of the posts, and the dew can all be smelled, seen, and felt. The poet has chosen particular images that paint a picture, but more than that, their exceptional clarity also helps you understand what the speaker is feeling. By using sensory images, concrete language, and exact words, the poet has helped you enter the scene that the speaker experienced after his father's death.

EXERCISE 1

Reread the poems in Group 1. Then use what you have learned in this lesson to answer these questions:

1. Find at least one sensory image from "In an Iridescent Time" that appeals to each of these senses: sight, hearing, touch.
2. Find five examples of concrete language in "Abandoned Farmhouse." Explain how the concrete language and images in the examples all help recreate the scene.

Now check your answers with your teacher. Review this part of the lesson if you don't understand why an answer was incorrect.

WRITING ON YOUR OWN 

Earlier in this unit you recorded sensory details about at least four moments during your day. Now you will focus on one particular moment and describe it more thoroughly. Follow these steps:

- Review the notes you recorded in your notebook. Does one situation seem more interesting than the rest? Do you remember one situation better than the others? Choose the one moment about which you feel you could write a short poem.

- Using your notes as a starting point, list every detail that you can remember from that moment. Set aside five separate note cards or pages, one for each sense—sight, smell, hearing, touch, and taste. On the appropriate card or page, list all the sensations that you felt at that particular moment.

LESSON 2 IMAGES AND MOOD

Every piece of writing conveys a mood. The term *mood* refers to the feeling that a piece evokes in a reader or the atmosphere that it helps to create. Sometimes the mood is obvious and intense, as in a ghost story or a love poem. At other times, the mood takes a back seat to the theme, the tone, or another element of the work.

In each of the poems in Group 2 the mood is clear. The poets have created these moods in a number of ways, including choosing their images carefully and using exact, concrete words. For example, in William Wordsworth's "I Wandered Lonely As a Cloud" the speaker is recalling an especially beautiful moment that occurred in a natural setting. The poem begins with an image that suggests a detached mood: "I wandered lonely as a cloud/That floats on high o'er vales and hills." The speaker is not connecting to his or her surroundings yet. However, the next few lines record a change of mood:

> When all at once I saw a crowd,
> A host, of golden daffodils;
> Beside the lake, beneath the trees,
> Fluttering and dancing in the breeze.

We can sense the speaker's mounting excitement at the surprising sight of the daffodils. The image of the cheerful daffodils suggests a liveliness and an intensity that contrasts with the speaker's original indifference. The poet then includes these joyful images relating to the golden flowers: "Continuous as the stars that shine/And twinkle on the milky way," "Ten thousand saw I at a glance,/Tossing their heads in sprightly dance," and "The waves beside them danced." The images clearly suggest a change in mood from detached and lonely to connected and happy.

The speaker in "The Proletariat Speaks" is just as intense as the speaker in Wordsworth's poem. The emotions she shares and the mood she creates, however, are quite different from the delight felt by the speaker in Wordsworth's poem. First the speaker paints pleasant mental pictures by describing beautiful things that she loves:

> I love beautiful things:
> Great trees, bending green winged branches to a velvet
> lawn,
> Fountains sparkling in white marble basins,
> Cool fragrance of lilacs and roses and honeysuckle.
> Or exotic blooms, filling the air with heart-contracting
> odors;
> Spacious rooms, cool and gracious with statues and books,
> Carven seats and tapestries, and old masters
> Whose patina shows the wealth of centuries.

Reading these lines you can see, hear, and smell the speaker's idea of the good life. Reality soon sets in, however, and your senses must cope with what the speaker actually deals with every day. Notice how the sensory images of her real life contrast with the images in her dream life:

> And so I work
> In a dusty office, whose grimèd windows
> Look out in an alley of unbelievable squalor,
> Where mangy cats, in their degradation, spurn
> Swarming bits of meat and bread;
> Where odors, vile and breathtaking, rise in fetid waves
> Filling my nostrils, scorching my humid, bitter cheeks.

The mood of this poem is frustrated and angry. The speaker is asking, "Why—when I love the finer things in life—am I forced to endure filth, bad food, and discomfort every day? It's not fair, and it's not right!" The images that the poet has chosen, both positive and negative, clearly contribute to the mood of the poem.

Not every poem has a mood as intense as the previous two poems. "Poem to Be Read at 3 A.M." quietly creates a contemplative, thoughtful mood. In it the speaker—a driver speeding past a sleeping town—spies a single light in a second-story window. First the speaker wonders what could be keeping the person in that house awake. Then he or she dedicates this short poem to the person in that room, who made the speaker feel less alone in the world. The comforting image of the single light shining in the night becomes a symbol, an object that stands for something larger than itself and which helps to convey the poem's mood.

EXERCISE 2

Reread "The Breathing." Then use what you have learned in this lesson to answer these questions:

1. How would you describe the mood of this poem? Which images contribute to that mood?
2. Of these images, "The river rushes down to the sea, tumbling over boulders on its way" and "The squirrels sleep undisturbed in their homes in the trees," which matches the mood of the poem better?

Now check your answers with your teacher. Review this part of the lesson if you don't understand why an answer was incorrect.

WRITING ON YOUR OWN

In this lesson you have seen that the careful choice of images helps poets communicate a mood. Now you will focus on images and how they affect your mood during your daily life. Follow these steps:

- People who work in the visual media, such as television, movies, and magazines, understand how powerful images can affect your mood. That is why they rely on images to influence your thinking and sell products. Set aside some time to watch television or look through a magazine. On a chart like the one below, record ten images that you see.
- Continue to fill out the chart by listing the sensory details that you associate with each image. For example, when you see a mother tucking a child into bed, you may imagine the child smelling the scent of her perfume or feeling the warmth and softness of the blanket.
- Finally, complete the chart by describing the mood that the image evoked in you or the one that you think the creators intended you to feel. Here is an example of one entry on the chart:

Image	Associated Sensory Details	Mood
white-water rafting	cold water spray, slapping of raft on the water	excitement

DISCUSSION GUIDES

1. Think about the way the speaker's feelings changed when he or she spied the "host of golden daffodils" in "I Wandered Lonely As a Cloud." Have you ever experienced a similar change of emotion after you saw a particular sight? Perhaps what you saw, instead of making you joyful, saddened or frightened you. Perhaps it made you laugh, or it surprised or inspired you. With a partner, discuss a time when an unexpected sight changed your mood. Explain how you felt both before and after you saw the sight.

2. In "The Breathing" Denise Levertov uses peaceful images to convey her mood as she describes a quiet, foggy night in the forest. If you were to describe a rainstorm in the forest, however, you would choose entirely different images to convey an entirely different mood. With a small group of classmates, create a list of images that you could use to describe either a rainstorm in the forest or a thunderstorm that breaks suddenly over a playground full of children. First identify the mood that you want to convey, and then brainstorm possible images that you could use to convey it. When you are finished, share your ideas with the rest of the class and see if you can compose a group poem about each kind of storm.

3. With a classmate, prepare an oral reading of "The Proletariat Speaks." The poem can easily be split into two speaking parts, the first part being the dreamlike listing of all the beautiful things that the speaker loves and the second part being the reality she experiences. Divide the parts between yourselves and alternate reading them. Be sure to let your voices reflect your feelings as you describe the dream world versus reality. Ideally, your listeners should have no trouble identifying the mood of the speakers from their tone of voice alone.

WRITE A POEM ABOUT A MOMENT

In this unit you have learned how poets create images and use them to convey a poem's mood. Now you will use what you have learned to write a poem of your own.

Follow these steps to write your poem. If you have questions about the writing process, refer to Using the Writing Process on page 245.

- Assemble and review the work you did for all the writing exercises in this unit: 1) a list of sensory details about at least four moments during the day, 2) five lists of sensations that you felt at a particular moment, 3) a chart listing media images and associated sensory details and moods.
- Recall the moment that you chose to write about in Writing on Your Own 1. Review the list of sensory details that you made at that time. Do you still want to write about that moment? If not, choose a different moment now and make another list of sensory details for your new choice. Then decide which mood you wish to convey.
- Decide whether you want your poem to rhyme or not. Remember that it is not important that it rhyme; the crucial element in this poem will be its use of images and concrete language to express a mood. Write the first draft of your poem, paying special attention to the appropriateness of the images you include. Be sure to use concrete language, including specific nouns and adjectives rather than general ones.
- Reread your poem several times but not all in the same sitting. If possible, give it a "cooling off" period and come back to it on another day. Does the poem effectively convey your chosen mood? Do the images you chose contribute to that mood? If necessary, make any changes at this time that will help make the poem's message and mood clearer. Consult with a classmate if you need another opinion.
- Proofread your poem for spelling, grammar, and formatting errors. Then make a clean copy and save it in your writing portfolio.

UNIT 4

Sounds in Poetry

Cool Tombs
by Carl Sandburg

Spring and Fall
by Gerard Manley Hopkins

truth
by Gwendolyn Brooks

The Burning
by N. Scott Momaday

Idaho
by Kaye Starbird

A narrow Fellow in the Grass
by Emily Dickinson

The Raven
by Edgar Allan Poe

Cargoes
by John Masefield

The Tyger
by William Blake

Shall I Compare Thee to a Summer's Day?
by William Shakespeare

INTRODUCTION

ABOUT THE LESSONS

When you read a daily newspaper, a textbook, or even a novel, there's rarely any advantage to reading it aloud. Almost always, you can understand the information in the text simply by reading the words silently to yourself. Reading a poem, however, is different. Often, reading the words silently gives you only a partial understanding. In order to truly understand the message of a poem, you often must read it aloud—even if only in your "mind's ear."

It is frequently impossible to express in words the sensory effects of the sounds in a poem. Nevertheless, we can at least identify some of the techniques a poet uses to create those effects. In this unit you will examine three ways in which poets use sounds to create music and meaning in their work. The first lesson will look at the repetition of consonant and vowel sounds in words. The second lesson will focus on rhyming patterns in poetry. The third lesson will examine rhythm, the patterns of stressed and unstressed syllables. The poems in this unit contain examples of these three types of sounds.

WRITING: USING SOUND EFFECTIVELY

In this unit you will learn how poets use both the repetition of sounds and rhythmic patterns to reinforce the meaning of their words. You also will use these techniques yourself. Your writing project during the unit will be to write four poems about the seasons, using the techniques you will study. At this time, begin collecting images of seasons that you can use in your poems. Here are some suggestions:

- Imagine taking photographs of nature at different times during each season. What plants, animals, and scenes would you try to catch on film? Create a chart like the one on the next page. In the first row, jot down several sights that you associate with each season.

	Winter	Spring	Summer	Fall
Things you might see				
Things you might hear				
Things you might smell				
Things you might taste				
Things you might touch and/or feel				

- Next, imagine taking a tape recorder outside and taping sounds that are typical of each season. What sounds might you hear and record? In the second row, write down some words that describe these sounds.
- Then think of things you might smell, taste, or touch—or that might touch you—during each season. For example, during fall you might smell burning leaves or taste apple cider. In winter you might feel cold, wet snow or hard, smooth ice; you also might shiver from the cold. In the third, fourth, and fifth rows write down some of the things you might smell, taste, and touch during each season.
- Save your chart. You will use it in future writing exercises.

ABOUT THIS POET

N. Scott Momaday was born in Lawton, Oklahoma, in 1934. His father is a respected Kiowa painter and art teacher, and his mother is a teacher and writer who is part Cherokee. Momaday received his undergraduate degree from the University of New Mexico and his master's and doctoral degrees from Stanford University. In addition to writing poetry and fiction, Momaday has taught English in various universities in the West and has also become known for his drawings and paintings.

Although Momaday is descended from Anglo-American ancestors as well as Kiowas and Cherokees, he feels a deeper connection with his Native American background. Momaday was brought up on the reservations of the Southwest and there came to appreciate the traditions of the Kiowa culture.

As a boy, Momaday was taught that there is no separation between the landscape of nature and the person who lives on it. He has said, "I believe that the Indian has an understanding of the physical world and of the earth as a spiritual entity that is his, very much his own. The non-Indian can benefit a good deal by having that perception revealed to him." Momaday's Pulitzer Prize–winning novel, *House Made of Dawn*, is the story of a war hero who returns to his reservation pueblo. The story explores the problems of straddling two worlds—the reservation and the white world.

Momaday seems to approach these problems with hope and a measure of confidence. He shows how Anglo-American and Native American traditions can coexist in his children's book *A Circle of Wonder: A Native American Christmas Story,* in which the spirit of a boy's grandfather visits him on Christmas Eve.

Momaday is proud of his heritage and feels that its rich spirituality gives him a distinct artistic advantage over non-Indian writers. In his poetry, novels, and short stories, he draws on its solidity, beauty, and strength.

AS YOU READ

As you read each poem in this unit, ask yourself the following questions:

- Is there any repetition of consonant and vowel sounds? If so, how does this repetition link words, phrases, or ideas? How does it add to the meaning or impact of the lines?
- Are there any rhymes and rhyming patterns?
- Does the poem's rhythm differ from normal conversation? If so, how? How does the rhythm contribute to the poem's meaning?

Cool Tombs

by Carl Sandburg

ABOUT THE SELECTION

Carl Sandburg (1878–1967) was and continues to be one of the most important modern poets in the United States. When his first book of poetry was published in 1916, he became a nationally known poet. His next major work was the first part of a six-volume biography of Abraham Lincoln. He won Pulitzer Prizes for both poetry and history. For more information about Sandburg, see About This Poet at the beginning of Unit 1. "Cool Tombs" combines the poet's love of history and his skill at writing poetry.

When Abraham Lincoln was shoveled into the tombs he forgot
the copperheads[1] and the assassin . . . in the dust, in the
cool tombs.

And Ulysses Grant lost all thought of con men and Wall Street,
cash and collateral[2] turned ashes . . . in the dust, in the cool
tombs.

Pocahontas' body, lovely as a poplar, sweet as a red haw[3] in
November or a pawpaw in May, did she wonder? does she
remember? . . . in the dust, in the cool tombs?

Take any streetful of people buying clothes and groceries,
cheering a hero or throwing confetti and blowing tin
horns . . . tell me if the lovers are losers . . . tell me if any
get more than the lovers . . . in the dust . . . in the cool
tombs.

---

[1] Northerners during the Civil War who sided with the South

[2] property used as security for a loan or other debt

[3] *haw* and *pawpaw* are the fruits of the hawthorn and pawpaw trees

Spring and Fall

by Gerard Manley Hopkins

ABOUT THE SELECTION

Around the year 1868, Gerard Manley Hopkins (1844–1889) burned most of his poems because he considered them a distraction from his religious calling. He was persuaded to return to writing later, however, and the poems he wrote show him to be one of the greatest—and most modern—of the Victorian poets. Hopkins was born in Essex, England. While a student at Cambridge University, he experienced a spiritual crisis that led him to become first a Catholic and then a Jesuit priest. Some time after he joined the Jesuit order, one of his superiors urged Hopkins to resume his writing. In his poetry he developed a technique that he called *sprung rhythm,* which emphasizes natural speech rhythms. As "Spring and Fall" shows, his poems also use the repetition of sounds extensively and effectively.

to a young child

Márgarét, áre you gríeving
Over Goldengrove unleaving?
Leáves líke the things of man, you
With your fresh thoughts care for, can you?
Ah! ás the heart grows older
It will come to such sights colder
By and by, nor spare a sigh
Though worlds of wanwood[1] leafmeal[2] lie;
And yet you will weep and know why.

---

[1] a word Hopkins made up to describe leaves, twigs, and such that fall from trees in autumn or as the trees age

[2] another word invented by Hopkins to suggest crushed, decaying leaves

Now no matter, child, the name:
Sórrow's spríngs áre the same.
Nor mouth had, no nor mind, expressed
What heart heard of, ghost[3] guessed:
It ís the blight[4] man was born for,
It is Margaret you mourn for.

[3] the spiritual part of a human; the soul

[4] something that interferes with growth or causes decay

truth

by Gwendolyn Brooks

ABOUT THE SELECTION

Gwendolyn Brooks (1917–) is an American poet who was the first African American to receive a Pulitzer Prize. She won the prize for her second book of poetry, *Annie Allen,* which tells about a black girl growing up in America during World War II. Born in Topeka, Kansas, Brooks grew up in Chicago and set many of her poems there. In 1968 she was named Poet Laureate (best poet) of Illinois. As you read "truth," notice how the sun is personified. What does it symbolize?

And if sun comes
How shall we greet him?
Shall we not dread him,
Shall we not fear him
After so lengthy a
Session with shade?

Though we have wept for him,
Though we have prayed
All through the night-years—
What if we wake one shimmering morning to
Hear the fierce hammering
Of his firm knuckles
Hard on the door?

Shall we not shudder?—
Shall we not flee
Into the shelter, the dear thick shelter
Of the familiar
Propitious[1] haze?

Sweet is it, sweet is it
To sleep in the coolness
Of snug unawareness.

The dark hangs heavily
Over the eyes.

[1] kindly; favorable

The Burning

by N. Scott Momaday

ABOUT THE SELECTION

N. Scott Momaday (1934–) is a poet, novelist, and artist who draws on his Kiowa and Cherokee heritage to create much of his work. He won the Pulitzer Prize for his novel *House Made of Dawn*, about a war hero who returns to his reservation pueblo. For more about Momaday, see About This Poet at the beginning of this unit. In "The Burning" Momaday paints a picture of impending devastation, as in wartime or at the end of the world.

In the numb, numberless days
There were disasters in the distance,
Strange upheavals. No one understood them.
At night the sky was scored[1] with light,
For the far planes[2] of the planet buckled and burned.
In the dawns were intervals of darkness
On the scorched sky, clusters of clouds and eclipse,[3]
And cinders descending.
Nearer in the noons
The air lay low and ominous and inert.[4]
And eventually at evening, or morning, or midday,
At the sheer wall of the wood,
Were shapes in the shadows approaching,
Always, and always alien and alike.
And in the foreground the fields were fixed in fire,
And the flames flowered in our flesh.

---

[1] marked with lines

[2] flat or level surfaces

[3] a temporary or permanent cutting off of light

[4] unable to move, or moving very slowly

Idaho

by Kaye Starbird

ABOUT THE SELECTION

Kaye Starbird, who began writing at the age of eight, has written poetry and novels for children and adults. She has sometimes published under the name C. S. Jennison. She once said that her ideas came from personal experience and from her "galloping imagination." In "Idaho" she gives some advice that combines both experience and imagination.

Farmers out in Idaho
Plant potatoes, row on row.
Then before the green vines show
Every farmer has to go
Daily hoe-ing with his hoe
Up and down the rows till—lo—
Finally potatoes grow.

This, potato farmers know:
What comes up must start below;
What you reap you have to sow;
What you grow you have to hoe.

If you don't like farming, though,
  And you've never *tried* a hoe
  Or you hate to guide a hoe
  Or you can't abide a hoe
  Stay away from Idaho.

A narrow Fellow in the Grass

by Emily Dickinson

ABOUT THE SELECTION

Emily Dickinson (1830–1886) was born in Amherst, Massachusetts, and was educated at Amherst Academy and Mount Holyoke Female Seminary. As a young woman, she withdrew from society. She spent most of the rest of her life inside her home, writing thousands of letters and poems. Fewer than ten of her poems were published during her lifetime. After her death, however, about 2,000 poems were found in the house and most of them have since been published. Dickinson is now considered one of America's major poets. She is noted for her use of unconventional capitalization and punctuation, figurative language, precise words, and complex rhythms and rhymes as well as her original, personal way of looking at life, death, and love. "A narrow Fellow in the Grass" focuses not so much on what the "narrow fellow" looks like but on how it acts and how the speaker reacts to it. Note the unique way in which the final line expresses the idea of shivering in fright.

A narrow Fellow in the Grass
Occasionally rides—
You may have met Him—did you not
His notice sudden is—

The Grass divides as with a Comb—
A spotted shaft[1] is seen—
And then it closes at your feet
And opens further on—

---

[1] the long, narrow body of an arrow, or an object having a similar shape

He likes a Boggy Acre
A Floor too cool for Corn—
Yet when a Boy, and Barefoot—
I more than once at Noon
Have passed, I thought, a Whip lash
Unbraiding in the Sun
When stooping to secure it
It wrinkled, and was gone—

Several of Nature's People
I know, and they know me—
I feel for them a transport[2]
Of cordiality[3]—

But never met this Fellow
Attended, or alone
Without a tighter breathing
And Zero at the Bone—

---

[2] the condition of being moved by emotion

[3] friendliness; warmth

The Raven

by Edgar Allan Poe

ABOUT THE SELECTION

Edgar Allan Poe (1809–1849) was one of the most influential writers in American literature. He wrote memorable horror stories, the first modern detective stories, ground-breaking literary criticism, and musical and hypnotic poems. He was born in Boston and was adopted at an early age by a Virginia merchant. In 1826 Poe enrolled in the University of Richmond, but he dropped out because of gambling debts. He was soon making his living by writing and editing. His first wife died in 1847, and two years later, while preparing for his second marriage, Poe died under mysterious circumstances.

"The Raven," published in 1845, is the poem that made Poe famous. In a later essay called "The Philosophy of Composition," Poe explained the process of writing this poem, stating that he concentrated on developing the emotional atmosphere rather than describing any specific event. Many of the words are used for their sounds and exotic flavor rather than their meanings.

Once upon a midnight dreary, while I pondered, weak and weary,
Over many a quaint and curious volume of forgotten lore,
While I nodded, nearly napping, suddenly there came a tapping,
As of some one gently rapping, rapping at my chamber door.
" 'Tis some visitor," I muttered, "tapping at my chamber door—
Only this, and nothing more."

Ah, distinctly I remember it was in the bleak December,
And each separate dying ember wrought its ghost upon the floor.
Eagerly I wished the morrow;—vainly I had sought to borrow
From my books surcease[1] of sorrow—sorrow for the lost Lenore—
For the rare and radiant maiden whom the angels name Lenore—
Nameless here for evermore.

And the silken sad uncertain rustling of each purple curtain
Thrilled me—filled me with fantastic terrors never felt before;
So that now, to still the beating of my heart, I stood repeating
" 'Tis some visitor entreating entrance at my chamber door;—
This it is, and nothing more."

Presently my soul grew stronger; hesitating then no longer,
"Sir," said I, "or Madam, truly your forgiveness I implore;
But the fact is I was napping, and so gently you came rapping,
And so faintly you come tapping, tapping at my chamber door,
That I scarce was sure I heard you"—here I opened wide the door;—
Darkness there, and nothing more.

---

[1] an end

Deep into that darkness peering, long I stood there
wondering, fearing,
Doubting, dreaming dreams no mortal ever dared to dream
before;
But the silence was unbroken, and the darkness gave no
token,
And the only word there spoken was the whispered word,
"Lenore!"
This I whispered, and an echo murmured back the word,
"Lenore!"—
Merely this, and nothing more.

Back into the chamber turning, all my soul within me
burning,
Soon I heard again a tapping somewhat louder than before.
"Surely," said I, "surely that is something at my window
lattice;
Let me see, then, what thereat is, and this mystery explore—
Let my heart be still a moment and this mystery explore;—
'Tis the wind and nothing more!"

Open here I flung the shutter, when, with many a flirt and
flutter,
In there stepped a stately raven of the saintly days of yore;
Not the least obeisance[2] made he; not an instant stopped or
stayed he;
But, with mien[3] of lord or lady, perched above my chamber
door—
Perched upon a bust of Pallas[4] just above my chamber door—
Perched, and sat, and nothing more.

---

[2] gesture to express respect, such as a curtsy or a bow

[3] manner or appearance

[4] another name for Athena, the Greek goddess of wisdom

[5] distracting the attention of; amusing

Then this ebony bird beguiling[5] my sad fancy into smiling,
By the grave and stern decorum of the countenance it wore,
"Though thy crest be shorn and shaven, thou," I said, "art
sure no craven,
Ghastly grim and ancient raven wandering from the Nightly
shore—
Tell me what thy lordly name is on the Night's Plutonian[6]
shore!"
Quoth the raven, "Nevermore."

Much I marvelled this ungainly fowl to hear discourse so
plainly,
Though its answer little meaning—little relevancy bore,
For we cannot help agreeing that no living human being
Ever yet was blessed with seeing bird above his chamber
door—
Bird or beast upon the sculptured bust above his chamber
door,
With such name as "Nevermore."

But the raven, sitting lonely on the placid bust, spoke only
That one word, as if his soul in that one word he did outpour.
Nothing farther then he uttered—not a feather then he
fluttered—
Till I scarcely more than muttered "Other friends have flown
before—
On the morrow *he* will leave me, as my hopes have flown
before."
Then the bird said "Nevermore."

Startled at the stillness broken by reply so aptly spoken,
"Doubtless," said I, "what it utters is its only stock and store
Caught from some unhappy master whom unmerciful Disaster
Followed fast and followed faster till his songs one burden
bore—
Till the dirges of his Hope that melancholy burden bore
Of 'Never—nevermore.' "

---

[6] relating to the god Pluto or to his land of the dead, the underworld

But the raven still beguiling all my sad soul into smiling,
Straight I wheeled a cushioned seat in front of bird and bust
and door;
Then, upon the velvet sinking, I betook myself to linking
Fancy unto fancy, thinking what this ominous bird of yore—
What this grim, ungainly, ghastly, gaunt, and ominous bird of
yore
Meant in croaking "Nevermore."

This I sat engaged in guessing, but no syllable expressing
To the fowl whose fiery eyes now burned into my bosom's
core;
This and more I sat divining, with my head at ease reclining
On the cushion's velvet lining that the lamplight gloated o'er,
But whose velvet violet lining with the lamplight gloating o'er,
She shall press, ah, nevermore!

Then, methought, the air grew denser, perfumed from an
unseen censer[7]
Swung by angels whose faint foot-falls tinkled on the tufted
floor.
"Wretch," I cried, "thy God hath lent thee—by these angels
he hath sent thee
Respite—respite and nepenthe[8] from thy memories of Lenore!
Quaff,[9] oh quaff this kind nepenthe and forget this lost
Lenore!"
Quoth the raven, "Nevermore."

---

7 vessel for burning incense

8 mythical drug that eases grief by erasing one's memory

9 drink heartily

"Prophet!" said I, "thing of evil!—prophet still, if bird or devil!—
Whether Tempter sent, or whether tempest tossed thee here ashore,
Desolate, yet all undaunted, on this desert land enchanted—
On this home by Horror haunted—tell me truly, I implore—
Is there—*is* there balm[10] in Gilead?—tell me—tell me, I implore!"
Quoth the raven, "Nevermore."

"Prophet!" said I, "thing of evil—prophet still, if bird or devil!
By that Heaven that bends above us—by that God we both adore—
Tell this soul with sorrow laden if, within the distant Aidenn,
It shall clasp a sainted maiden whom the angels name Lenore—
Clasp a rare and radiant maiden whom the angels name Lenore."
Quoth the raven, "Nevermore."

"Be that word our sign of parting, bird or fiend!" I shrieked, upstarting—
"Get thee back into the tempest and the Night's Plutonian shore!
Leave no black plume as a token of that lie thy soul hath spoken!
Leave my loneliness unbroken!—quit the bust above my door!
Take thy beak from out my heart, and take thy form from off my door!"
Quoth the raven, "Nevermore."

---

[10] soothing lotion or oil

And the raven, never flitting, still is sitting, still is sitting
On the pallid bust of Pallas just above my chamber door;
And his eyes have all the seeming of a demon's that is dreaming,
And the lamp-light o'er him streaming throws his shadow on the floor;
And my soul from out that shadow that lies floating on the floor
Shall be lifted—nevermore!

Cargoes

by John Masefield

ABOUT THE SELECTION

John Masefield (1878–1967) was born in Ledbury, Herefordshire, England. He was apprenticed as a sailor when he was 13 years old. After four years at sea, on sailing ships, tramp steamers, and ocean liners, he became a writer. In addition to poetry, Masefield wrote novels, plays, and literary criticism—more than 100 books in all. He was England's poet laureate from 1930 until his death.

"Cargoes" talks about three ships used in different centuries. A *quinquireme* was a large ship used in ancient times for trade and warfare and powered by five banks of rowing men. A *galleon* was a large Spanish sailing ship of the 1400s and 1500s, with three or four decks. A *coaster* is a modern ship that stays close to the coast, carrying passengers or cargo from port to port.

Quinquireme of Nineveh from distant Ophir
Rowing home to haven in sunny Palestine,
With a cargo of ivory,
And apes and peacocks,
Sandalwood, cedarwood, and sweet white wine.

Stately Spanish galleon coming from the Isthmus,
Dipping through the Tropics by the palm-green shores,
With a cargo of diamonds,
Emeralds, amethysts,
Topazes, and cinnamon, and gold moidores.[1]
Dirty British coaster with a salt-caked smoke stack
Butting through the Channel in the mad March days,
With a cargo of Tyne coal,
Road-rail, pig-lead,
Firewood, iron-ware, and cheap tin trays.

---

[1] gold coins used before the 1800s

The Tyger

by William Blake

ABOUT THE SELECTION

William Blake (1757–1827) was a brilliant writer and artist whose beliefs were so unusual that during his life he was often considered insane. Born in London, he was apprenticed at age 14 as an engraver, beginning a career as an engraver and book illustrator. He printed most of the poems he wrote on engraved copper plates and then hand-colored the illustrations. Much of Blake's poetry presents his belief that what humans learn through the senses is incomplete or inaccurate. Instead, he says, we should rely on instinct and imagination. His best-known works are *Songs of Innocence* (1789) and *Songs of Experience* (1794), which present symbols of what Blake called "the two contrary states of the human soul." "The Tyger" is from *Songs of Experience.*

Tyger Tyger, burning bright,
In the forests of the night;
What immortal hand or eye,
Could frame thy fearful symmetry?[1]

In what distant deeps or skies
Burnt the fire of thine eyes!
On what wings dare he aspire?
What the hand dare seize the fire?

[1] having matching form or shape on both sides of a central dividing line; beauty as a result of that balance

And what shoulder, & what art,
Could twist the sinews[2] of thy heart?
And when thy heart began to beat,
What dread hand? & what dread feet?

What the hammer? what the chain,
In what furnace was thy brain?
What the anvil? what dread grasp,
Dare its deadly terrors clasp?

When the stars threw down their spears
And water'd heaven with their tears:
Did he smile his work to see?
Did he who made the Lamb make thee?

Tyger, Tyger burning bright,
In the forests of the night:
What immortal hand or eye,
Dare frame thy fearful symmetry?

[2] tendons; strength

Shall I Compare Thee to a Summer's Day?

by William Shakespeare

ABOUT THE SELECTION

William Shakespeare (1564–1616) is widely considered the greatest playwright of all time and the finest poet to use the English language. He was born in Stratford-upon-Avon in England and was educated in grammar schools there. He became an actor and playwright in London, then a shareholder in a popular company of actors that often performed for Queen Elizabeth I and, later, James I. Shakespeare is best known for his plays, including comedies, tragedies, and historical plays, all written in blank verse, a form of unrhymed poetry. He also wrote more than 150 sonnets, of which the poem presented here is the most popular.

Shall I compare thee to a summer's day?
Thou art more lovely and more temperate:[1]
Rough winds do shake the darling buds of May,
And summer's lease hath all too short a date;
Sometime too hot the eye of heaven shines,
And often is his gold complexion dimm'd;
And every fair[2] from fair sometime declines,
By chance or nature's changing course untrimm'd:
But thy eternal summer shall not fade
Nor lose possession of that fair thou ow'st;[3]
Nor shall Death brag thou wand'rest in his shade,
When in eternal lines to time thou grow'st;
    So long as men can breathe or eyes can see,
    So long lives this, and this gives life to thee.

---

[1] neither hot nor cold; pleasant; moderate

[2] a beautiful woman; loveliness, beauty (obsolete meaning)

[3] own; have (obsolete meaning)

UNDERSTANDING THE POEMS

Record your answers to these questions in your personal literature notebook. Follow the directions for each group.

GROUP 1

Reread the poems in Group 1 to complete these sentences.

Reviewing the Selection

1. The poem in Group 1 that talks about Abraham Lincoln is
   a. "Spring and Fall."
   b. "Cool Tombs."
   c. "The Burning."
   d. "truth."

Interpreting the Selection

2. In "truth" *shade* and *darkness* stand for
   a. the end of the world.
   b. ignorance.
   c. coolness.
   d. death.

3. The speaker in "Spring and Fall" recognizes that the real reason for Margaret's tears is that
   a. she hates to see bright autumn leaves fall.
   b. the weather is getting cold.
   c. she sees that everything—herself included—must die.
   d. she has seen a ghost.

Recognizing How Words Are Used

4. Of the following lines from "The Burning," the one that shows the *most* repetition of the /f/ sound is
   a. "There were disasters in the distance, . . ."
   b. "For the far planes of the planet buckled and burned."
   c. "And in the foreground the fields were fixed in fire, . . ."
   d. "And the flames flowered in our flesh."

Appreciating Poetry

5. The message of "Cool Tombs" is that death
   a. makes everyone equal.
   b. is to be feared as a terrible disaster.
   c. will never frighten those who live good lives.
   d. comes when you least expect it.

GROUP 2

Reread the poems in Group 2 to complete these sentences.

Reviewing the Selection

6. Once, when the speaker in "A narrow Fellow in the Grass" saw a long, coiled snake, he or she thought it was
a. a comb.
b. some long grass that had been braided.
c. a whip lash left in the field.
d. a bone.

7. The speaker in "The Raven" says that a strange bird has made his home on
a. a statue in the speaker's room.
b. a statue in the park.
c. the Plutonian shore.
d. a cushioned seat with velvet violet lining.

Interpreting the Selection

8. In "A narrow Fellow in the Grass" the phrase "Zero at the Bone" refers to
a. the fact that a snake has no bony skeleton.
b. the cold feeling the speaker has whenever he or she sees a snake.
c. the fact that the speaker has never actually touched a snake.
d. none of the above.

Recognizing How Words Are Used

9. In "The Raven" the poetic technique(s) contained in the line "Caught from some unhappy master whom unmerciful Disaster" is
a. internal rhyme.
b. alliteration (repetition of selected consonant sounds).
c. assonance (repetition of selected vowel sounds).
d. all of the above.

Appreciating Poetry

10. The author's purpose in "Idaho" is to
a. amuse the reader.
b. teach something about farming.
c. praise farmers.
d. express a personal opinion about potatoes.

GROUP 3

Reread the poems in Group 3 to complete these sentences.

Reviewing the Selection

11. In "Shall I Compare Thee to a Summer's Day?" the phrase "the eye of heaven" refers to
   a. the sun.
   b. the moon.
   c. the North Star.
   d. the Evening Star.

12. "Cargoes" describes a modern ship as
   a. rowing home to haven.
   b. traveling past palm-green shores.
   c. carrying a cargo of jewels.
   d. butting through the Channel.

Interpreting the Selection

13. The speaker in "Cargoes" says that in comparison with the ships of ancient times, the ships of modern times
   a. are much bigger.
   b. are not attractive.
   c. move faster.
   d. carry more natural resources for trade.

Recognizing How Words Are Used

14. In "Shall I Compare Thee to a Summer's Day?" the line "And every fair from fair sometime declines" means that
   a. not every woman would ask to go to a fair.
   b. an attractive woman can't be the most beautiful one of every group.
   c. every beautiful woman eventually loses her beauty.
   d. not every woman would ask to be beautiful.

Appreciating Poetry

15. The tone of "The Tyger" is best described as
   a. logical and detached.
   b. calm and contented.
   c. confident and assertive.
   d. awestruck and fearful.

Now check your answers with your teacher. Study the questions you answered incorrectly. What types of questions were they? Talk with your teacher about ways to work on those skills.

Sounds in Poetry

On a night when you have insomnia, you might tune your radio to a program that will help make you sleepy. Given a choice of music, you'll probably tune to an "easy listening" station rather than one with lively dance music. If all you can find is talk radio, you're more likely to choose a program about a topic you are uninterested in and whose participants are speaking in softer, more monotonous voices. In short, you are looking for sounds that are soothing, not jarring; sounds that are undemanding and have no surprises.

Poets are not interested in putting their readers to sleep. Even when they wish to soothe their readers, they want them alert and thinking. Therefore, knowing the effects of monotonous sound, they make sure their words demand attention, are surprising, and are full of variations in sound. The lessons in this unit will examine some of the sound techniques that poets use to put interest and impact into their words:

1. Poets repeat selected consonant and vowel sounds to link words or ideas, to draw attention to particular words, and to suggest particular moods.
2. Many poets create interesting sound patterns with rhyming words.
3. Many poets arrange their words to produce a regular rhythm. They also then vary the rhythm to keep it from sounding monotonous.

LESSON 1 ALLITERATION, ASSONANCE, AND CONSONANCE

Perform this experiment: Without thinking of the meaning of the following lines from "Cool Tombs" and "The Burning," read them aloud or move your mouth to form the words as you read silently. Concentrate on what your mouth, tongue, lips, and teeth are doing. How does the shape of your mouth change? Is your tongue lying still or moving from front to back or up and down? When is your mouth open? When do you bring your lips together or touch your teeth to your lips?

> And Ulysses Grant lost all thought of con men and Wall
> Street, cash and collateral turned ashes . . . in the dust,
> in the cool tombs.
>
> And in the foreground the fields were fixed in fire,
> And the flames flowered in our flesh.

Reading the first excerpt, your mouth was open most of the time. It closed only when you pronounced the letter *m* in *men* and *tombs*. For the second set of lines, however, you had to bring your lower lip to your top teeth repeatedly, every time you made the /f/ sound. For the last seven words of the first excerpt, the inside of your mouth took only two positions. Only your tongue moved to make the sounds as you read *in the dust, in the*. Then, after your mouth changed shape for the /oo/ sound of cool, it kept that shape for tombs. Contrast that lack of motion with the increase in your mouth's motions as you read the last seven words of the second excerpt. Your mouth changed shape at *flames*, at the first and second syllables of *flowered*, at *in*, at the second vowel sound of *our*, and at *flesh*. Even without a thought about the words you are saying, you can feel the contrast between the peacefulness of the first excerpt and the rapid changes of the second.

Readers would not enjoy reading poetry if they had to concentrate on mouth movements as you did in this experiment. But this activity helps you become aware of the physical effects of sound changes on readers. You can more easily understand the impact of the vowel and consonant sounds that a poet chooses, as well as the impact of the repetition of those sounds. You also can understand now why poetry is meant to be read aloud.

As you learned in Unit 1, the repetition of a sound, usually a consonant sound, is called *alliteration*. Some critics limit the definition of alliteration to the repetition of beginning sounds. Certainly, alliteration is most noticeable when the repeated sound is at the beginning of several words, as the /f/ sound was in the above lines from "The Burning." It is useful, however, to be aware of alliterative sounds anywhere in a word or words. For example, you can say that there is alliteration of both the /s/ and /z/ sounds, as well as the /d/ and /t/ sounds, in the phrase "disasters in the distance."

The repetition of a vowel sound, particularly in stressed syllables, is called *assonance*. In assonance, a vowel sound is repeated, but the consonant sounds following the vowel are different, as in the phrase *clean sweep*. It is generally easier to determine assonance by listening to the words than by looking for similar spellings. Note, for example, the two different spellings of the /oo/ sound in *cool* and *tombs*.

Consonance is the repetition of a consonant sound at the end of stressed syllables with different vowel sounds. Examples in the excerpts above include the repeated /n/ sound in *con men* and the repeated /nd/ sound in *and, turned*.

Even poets who do not use rhyme or a formal rhythm usually take advantage of the power of alliteration, assonance, and consonance. When these techniques are used along with patterns of rhyme and rhythm, they add another layer of rich sound effects to a poem. For an illustration of this richness, read these excerpts from "Spring and Fall." In them, the letters indicating repeated vowel and consonant sounds are underlined:

> Márgarét, áre you gríeving
> Over Goldengrove unleaving? . . . .
>
> Nor mouth had, no nor mind, expressed
> What heart heard of, ghost guessed:
> It ís the blight man was born for,
> It is Margaret you mourn for.

EXERCISE 1

Reread the poems in Group 1. Then use what you have learned in this lesson to answer these questions:

1. Copy lines 6–8 of "The Burning," leaving a line of space above and below each line. Underscore the letters and letter combinations that represent repeated consonant sounds. Then list all the instances of alliteration that you find in these lines.

2. The poem "truth" has five stanzas of varying lengths, without a regular pattern of rhythm or rhyme. Alliteration and assonance help to unify each stanza. For each stanza, identify at least one of these vowel and consonant sounds that is repeated in the stanza frequently enough to link the lines: long *e;* the sound of *er/ir/ur;* the vowel sound in *ear;* and the /d/, /h/, /l/, /m/, /s/, /sh/, /v/, and /w/ sounds. After the sound, list the words in the stanza that include it.

Now check your answers with your teacher. Review this part of the lesson if you don't understand why an answer was incorrect.

WRITING ON YOUR OWN 

You have seen how poets use the repetition of vowel and consonant sounds to emphasize meaning, link words, and produce a melody in a poem. Now you will use the repetition of sounds as you write a short poem about a season. Follow these steps:

- Refer to the chart of sensory images that you created for the introductory writing exercise. Choose one season to begin working with and then select from one to three images to describe in your poem.
- Your object is to write a four-line poem that contains no rhyme or regular rhythm. As you consider words to use in describing

the selected images, think of both their meanings and their sounds. As you write, make sure you include examples of alliteration, assonance, and consonance. Try to highlight important words with these sound techniques.

- In your poem you may decide to imitate a particular sound that can be heard during the season, such as the buzzing of bees in spring. This technique is called *onomatopoeia*. For this, you might use made-up words or nonsense syllables.
- When you have written your short poem, meet with one or two classmates to share what you have all written and to comment on each other's writing. Use suggestions from your writing group to improve your poem. Then make a clean copy of your poem and save it, along with your chart, for the next writing exercise.

LESSON 2 RHYME AND RHYME PATTERNS

As you know, rhyming words are words whose final vowel and consonant sounds are the same. There are several types of rhyme, including *end* or *internal rhyme*, *masculine* or *feminine rhyme*, and *near-rhyme*.

Two lines of poetry have *end rhyme* when they end with words that rhyme. This example is from "Idaho":

> Farmers out in Idaho
> Plant potatoes, row on row.

If the rhyming words are within a single line, the line has *internal rhyme*. This example is from "The Raven":

> Once upon a midnight dreary, while I pondered,
> weak and weary,

If two rhyming words are only one syllable long, or only their final, stressed syllables have matching end sounds, we call the rhyme *masculine rhyme:*

/ ∪ /
Farmers out in Ida<u>ho</u>
/
Plant potatoes, row on <u>row</u>.

If the rhyming words have a stressed syllable followed by one or more unstressed syllables, we call the rhyme *feminine rhyme:*

/ ∪
Once upon a midnight <u>dreary</u>, while I pondered,
/ ∪
weak and <u>weary</u>,

In *near-rhyme*, the two words have matching consonant sounds (consonance), or matching vowel sounds (assonance), but not both. This example is from "A narrow Fellow in the Grass":

The Grass divides as with a Comb—
A spotted shaft is see<u>n</u>—
And then it closes at your feet
And opens further <u>on</u>—

The *near-rhyme* is found in the words *seen* and *on*, which both end in the letter *n* following different vowel sounds.

In addition to feminine rhyme, which involves just one stressed syllable and additional unstressed syllables, there are rhymes with several stressed syllables. These attention-demanding rhymes are usually limited to humorous poems, such as "Idaho":

If you don't like farming, though,
And you've never *<u>tried</u>* <u>a</u> <u>hoe</u>
Or you hate to <u>guide</u> <u>a</u> <u>hoe</u>
Or you can't a <u>bide</u> <u>a</u> <u>hoe</u>
Stay away from <u>Idaho</u>.

When describing a poem, it is usually necessary to describe its pattern of rhyming words, or *rhyme scheme*. To do so, match a single letter with each end sound and reuse the letter when that end sound repeats. Continue until you have written a letter for each line in the stanza. For example, the rhyme scheme for the last stanza of "Idaho" is simply *aaaaa* because each line ends with the same sound. For more information about rhyme schemes see Unit 6.

EXERCISE 2

Reread the poems in Group 2. Then use what you have learned in this lesson to answer these questions:

1. "A narrow Fellow in the Grass" uses both near-rhyme and masculine rhyme. In a stanza other than stanza 2, identify two or more words at the ends of lines that show the same type of near-rhyme as the stanza 2 sample on page 135. Then identify which stanzas use masculine rhyme.
2. What is the rhyme scheme of "The Raven"? For this exercise consider only end rhyme. Write the rhyme scheme for a typical stanza.
3. Examine stanza 5 of "The Raven." One line ends with the word *token.* Find rhymes for *token* in two other places in this stanza. Compare stanza 5 with other stanzas of the poem. Does Poe use this unusual pattern of rhyming words elsewhere? If so, where?

Now check your answers with your teacher. Review this part of the lesson if you don't understand why an answer was incorrect.

WRITING ON YOUR OWN 

In this exercise you will make use of rhyme in writing a second short poem about a season. Follow these steps:

- Review your chart of sensory details related to the different seasons. You already have written a poem about one of the four seasons. Now choose a second season and write a poem about it that is six or more lines long and uses rhyme.
- Beginning with the words already on your chart, brainstorm rhyming words that might be useful in describing your chosen season. For example, if you have chosen fall, your chart may include *colored leaves* and *cold nights*. For the word *leaves,* your brainstorming might produce the rhyming words *heaves, believes,* and *sleeves* and the near-rhymes *red, said,* and *instead.* For *cold*, you might brainstorm *gold, old,* and *told;* and for *night,* you might brainstorm *sight, right, flight, white,* and *bite.*
- Write your poem. As you organize your ideas and words, try to create a rhyme scheme more complex than simply *aa bb cc*. For example, you might consider *abc abc* or *ab cb db*. Whether you make your rhythms regular or not is your decision.
- When you have finished your poem, meet with one or two classmates to read and comment on each other's work. Use suggestions from your writing group to improve your poem. Then make a clean copy of your poem and save it, along with your chart and your first poem, for the next writing exercise.

LESSON 3 RHYTHM

Every spring, people in the Northern Hemisphere know that the days will lengthen. Every fall, people in the northern half of the United States expect leaves to change color and eventually fall. These are some of the natural rhythms of the year. They are repeating, regular patterns.

In poetry, *rhythm* refers to patterns of stressed syllables. Like speech, all poetry has rhythms, but the rhythms are not always regular. Below is an example of a regular rhythm. Its stressed, or accented, syllables are marked with a slanted line (/). Its unstressed syllables are marked with a curved line (∪). As you read this stanza from William Blake's "The Tyger," note how the stressed and unstressed syllables alternate:

/∪ /∪ /∪ /
Tyger Tyger, burning bright,
/ ∪ /∪ / ∪ /
In the forests of the night;
/ ∪ /∪ / ∪ /
What immortal hand or eye,
∪ / ∪ /∪ /∪ /
Could frame thy fearful symmetry?

In the English language, natural speech patterns tend toward fairly regular rhythms. Therefore, some poets prefer to use conversational rhythms, without trying to alternate stressed and unstressed syllables in a specific pattern. The poems these poets write are called *free verse*. For examples in Group 1, see "Cool Tombs," "The Burning," and "truth."

Poets who prefer to use specific rhythms have a limited number of basic patterns, or *feet* (measures with at least one stressed syllable), available. In fact, most critics and poets recognize no more than five patterns: 1) two stressed syllables (a stressed syllable by itself), 2) a single unstressed syllable *before* a stressed syllable, 3) a single unstressed syllable *after* a stressed syllable, 4) two unstressed syllables *before* a stressed syllable, and 5) two unstressed syllables *after* a stressed syllable. In "The Tyger" Blake uses four feet per line. Three out of the four are *trochee feet*, in which a stressed syllable is followed by a single unstressed syllable.

With only five basic patterns, you might expect that poets would repeat themselves and that new poems would sound a great deal like old poems. Poets avoid this possibility by such techniques as changing the number of feet in selected lines, alternating the basic patterns, and allowing minor variations in a single pattern. This gives some poems such complicated rhythms that it is difficult to pin them down to everyone's satisfaction. Examine, for example, this stanza of "Cargoes." More of the stanza's feet are trochee than anything else. But they are so combined with other rhythmic feet and extra syllables that the rhythm of this poem is totally unlike that of "The Tyger."

> /∪ /∪ /∪ ∪ ∪ / ∪ / ∪
> Dirty British coaster with a salt-caked smoke stack
> /∪ / ∪ / ∪ ∪ ∪ / / /
> Butting through the Channel in the mad March days,
> ∪ ∪ /∪ ∪ / ∪
> With a cargo of Tyne coal,
> / ∪ / ∪
> Road-rail, pig-lead,
> / ∪ /∪ / ∪ / / /
> Firewood, iron-ware, and cheap tin trays.

Without question, lines 1, 2, and 5 have more stressed syllables than the two stressed syllables in lines 3 and 4. Notice how stressed syllables are separated by one, two, or no unstressed syllables. Despite this apparently random mixture of patterns, poet John Masefield has complete control of the rhythm. There is a music and flow to the lines, with the three stressed syllables at the end of the stanza providing a strong close. For more information about rhythmic patterns in poetry see Unit 6.

EXERCISE 3

Reread "Shall I Compare Thee to a Summer's Day?" Then use what you have learned in this lesson to answer these questions:

1. **Copy the last two lines of the poem, leaving a line of space above and below each line. Then draw a slanted line (/) above**

every stressed syllable. Do both lines have the same number of feet (measures with a stressed syllable)? Tell how many feet there are in each line.

2. Draw a curved line (◡) above every unstressed syllable. Keeping in mind that there may be some feet that do not match the general pattern, determine which of the five patterns described in this lesson are used in the poem.

Now check your answers with your teacher. Review this part of the lesson if you don't understand why an answer was incorrect.

WRITING ON YOUR OWN 

In this lesson you have examined rhythmic patterns in poems. Now you will write a short poem that makes use of a regular rhythm. Follow these steps:

- Review your chart of sensory images and then choose one of the two remaining seasons. Write a poem about that season that is at least two lines long and that follows the same rhythm as "Shall I Compare Thee to a Summer's Day?"
- In Exercise 3 above you marked the stressed and unstressed syllables in the last lines of the poem by Shakespeare. Reread those lines to get the rhythm into your head. Then select an image from your chart and write several phrases about it in words that fit the rhythm. Mark the stressed and unstressed syllables in your phrases and compare the pattern with those on your lines from "Shall I Compare Thee to a Summer's Day?" You should have five feet (measures) in each line, and each foot should have one unstressed syllable and one stressed syllable. Replace and add to your words until you have at least two lines of verse that tell one or more complete thoughts. Your lines need not rhyme.

- When you have finished your poem, meet with one or two classmates to read and comment on each other's work. Use your classmates' suggestions to improve your poem. Then make a clean copy of your poem and save it, along with your chart and your other two poems, for the next writing exercise.

DISCUSSION GUIDES

1. Several poems in this unit develop a mood of awe, fear, or mystery. Which poems would you place in this group? Do you suppose the poet intended to send chills down readers' spines? If so, why might he or she have chosen to do so? What characteristics can you identify that contribute to the mood created by these poems? Work with a small group to draw up a list of the unsettling poems in the unit and the characteristics that make them unsettling.

2. "A narrow Fellow in the Grass," "The Raven," and "The Tyger" are all poems about animals. Which poem describes its subject most realistically? Which describes it least realistically? Do any of the poets intend the animal to represent, or symbolize, something other than a creature in nature? If so, what does the animal symbolize? Compare these three poems in a whole-group discussion. Can you come to some agreement on answers to these questions?

3. Review the poems "Spring and Fall," "Cool Tombs," and "Shall I Compare Thee to a Summer's Day?" and analyze what they say about death. Do the poems share a common attitude or do they disagree? Support your opinion with lines from the poems.

4. Select a short poem from this unit to present to all or part of the class. Take a day to practice reading the poem with expression. If it is short, try to memorize it. Then perform the poem.

WRITE A POEM SEQUENCE

In this unit you have examined the sounds of poems and have applied sound techniques to some poems of your own. Now you will complete your series of poems about the seasons by writing a poem that uses repetition, rhyme, and rhythm.

Follow these steps to write your poem. If you have questions about the writing process, refer to Using the Writing Process on page 245.

- Assemble the work you did for all the writing exercises in this unit: 1) a chart of sensory details associated with the four seasons; 2) a poem about one season that uses alliteration, assonance, and consonance; 3) a poem about a second season that uses a definite rhyme scheme; 4) a poem about a third season that uses a definite rhythm.
- For this exercise you will write a poem that is at least 12 lines long and has at least 2 stanzas. The poem must make use of rhyme, a regular rhythm, and the repetition of vowel and consonant sounds. Review your chart of sensory details for the final remaining season. If you have enough material there for a 12-line poem, limit your topic to that single season. If you think you won't have enough to say, your poem could be about both that season and the year as a whole. For example, you could write 4 lines about the season and the other 8 lines about the year. As needed, review your chart of sensory details for the year.
- Select the images you want to describe and write your poem. Write as many stanzas as you need.
- Once more, share your poem with writing partners and follow their suggestions for improvement.
- Reread your poem one last time. Is the description of the season (and year) easy to understand and picture? Did you use alliteration and assonance at least a few times each? Is the rhyme scheme clear? Is the rhythm fairly regular? Make any additions and changes that are needed.
- Proofread your poem for spelling, grammar, and formatting errors. Then make a final copy and put it with your other three poems about the seasons. If you'd like, make a cover page for your collection. After sharing your work with the rest of the class, save it in your writing portfolio.

Figurative Language

The Waning Moon
by Percy Bysshe Shelley

Metaphor
by Eve Merriam

Song of the Sky Loom
Tewa Indian prayer,
translated by Herbert J. Spinden

When I Hear Your Name
by Gloria Fuertes, translated by Ada Long
and Philip Levine

Death, Be Not Proud
by John Donne

March 1st
by Kathleen Spivack

Birthday
by M. T. Buckley

Tiburón
by Martín Espada

Fall, leaves, fall
by Emily Brontë

INTRODUCTION

ABOUT THE LESSONS

Poetry aims to describe experiences vividly and express feelings strongly in as few words as possible. One of the most effective means of achieving that goal is through making comparisons. A poet who says that unfamiliar Object A is like familiar Object B leads readers to transfer knowledge and feelings about Object B to Object A. Now the poet doesn't have to describe Object A at all! It's a great trick if you can do it, but it is not always easy.

In this unit you will look at some of the ways in which poets make comparisons that clue readers in to some important characteristics shared by two people or things. First, you will focus on different types of comparisons, or figures of speech. Then you will consider how these comparisons express the messages and feelings that poets want to share. Unlike rhyme, rhythm, and other effects that depend on specific sounds, figures of speech can be reproduced in different languages. Sample poems for this unit, therefore, include two translations.

WRITING: USING FIGURES OF SPEECH

The poems in this unit present highly personal views of common experiences such as being born, noticing nature, looking at city streets, working, and dying. Each of the poets lets us know that he or she is an individual who doesn't merely accept others' attitudes or points of view. At the end of the unit you, too, will write a poem that reflects your personal views. At this time, begin to think of topics and themes about which you have strong feelings. Here are some suggestions:

- Do you have strong opinions about any particular topic? What topics can provoke you to start an argument or give an impromptu speech? For at least a day, carry around a notepad or paper and record your "hot topics." Every time you find yourself getting stirred up, jot down the situation or the topic under discussion.

- Are there any people who have made strong impressions on you, either favorably or unfavorably? What people do you remember vividly from your childhood? Why? What sets these individuals apart from everyone else in your memory? Take a few minutes to reflect on these questions. For each person you recall, list several reasons and/or details that come to mind readily. Limit your list to no more than five people.
- What kinds of weather affect your ability to function? What recurring events bring out anticipation or dread in you? Which of your possessions would you defend most strongly and hold on to long after they stop being useful? List a half-dozen events or objects that make you react with strong feeling when you think about them.
- Save your lists. You will use them later in the unit.

ABOUT THIS POET

Emily Brontë (1818–1848) was one of three sisters who became famous for their romantic and emotional novels. Emily was the middle sister, between Charlotte (1816–1855) and Anne (1820–1849). Their father was the parish clergyman in the small, isolated town of Haworth on the moors of Yorkshire, England. After their mother died in 1821, the girls and their brother Branwell were brought up by their aunt. She did her duty, but without affection, and sent the children to boarding schools as soon as they came of age. The schools gave the girls a better education than most girls of their time received, but they were harsh and uncomfortable places where all three sisters were unhappy.

The only jobs open to educated women of that era were schoolteacher and governess. Although the sisters held such jobs for short periods after leaving school, they spent most of their lives in the family home. They were shy and far from social activities, so they busied themselves with music, drawing, reading, and writing. In 1846 they published a book of poetry. To overcome the prejudices of the day against female writers, they used the pen names Currer, Ellis, and Acton Bell. Nevertheless, the poetry volume did not sell. The following year, however, each of the three sisters published a successful novel.

The novel that Charlotte published in 1847 was *Jane Eyre*, scandalous but wildly popular at the time and now recognized as a classic. Its heroine survives a cruel boarding school, becomes governess to the ward of a mysterious man, and almost marries her employer before learning he is already married. Anne's novel, *Agnes Grey*, was a less intense story along similar lines.

Emily's novel was *Wuthering Heights*, an even more emotional tale of forbidden love. Its hero and heroine, Heathcliff and Cathy, fall wildly in love but cannot marry because Heathcliff belongs to a lower class than Cathy. Out of revenge, he determines to destroy her family. Although Cathy tries to be a faithful wife to another man, she cannot control her passion for Heathcliff. At first *Wuthering Heights* was condemned for its immorality and violence. Today, however, it is regarded as a masterpiece. It was Emily Brontë's only novel. She died the year after it was published, at only 30 years of age.

AS YOU READ

As you read the poems in this unit, ask yourself the following questions:

- What unusual comparisons, or figures of speech, does the poet use? What characteristics do things or people being compared have in common? How does the poet phrase the comparison to point out those common characteristics?
- How do the figures of speech in the poem help express the theme?

The Waning Moon

by Percy Bysshe Shelley

ABOUT THE SELECTION

English poet Percy Bysshe Shelley (1792–1822) was one of the great writers of lyric poems (short poems expressing strong emotion). He was born into a wealthy family and began studies at Eton College, but he was expelled in 1811 for a publication in which he defended atheism. Many of his poems present his belief that spiritual truth can be understood only through the imagination. In addition to a great amount of poetry, Shelley also wrote important literary criticism. His second wife, Mary Wollstonecraft Shelley, also gained fame as a writer for her novel *Frankenstein.* Shelley drowned in a sailing accident in Italy. In the six lines of his poem "The Waning Moon" notice the definite mood he establishes.

And like a dying lady, lean and pale,
Who totters forth, wrapped in a gauzy veil,
Out of her chamber, led by the insane
And feeble wanderings of her fading brain,
The moon arose up in the murky East,
A white and shapeless mass.

Metaphor

by Eve Merriam

ABOUT THE SELECTION

Eve Merriam (1916–1992) wrote plays, fiction, biographies, and most importantly, poetry for adults and children. In her second collection of poems for children, *It Doesn't Always Have to Rhyme* (1964), she included poems on many of the elements of poetry, including "Simile," "Onomatopoeia," and the following poem, "Metaphor."

Morning is
a new sheet of paper
for you to write on.

Whatever you want to say,
all day,
until night
folds it up
and files it away.

The bright words and the dark words
are gone
until dawn
and a new day
to write on.

Song of the Sky Loom

Tewa Indian prayer, translated by Herbert J. Spinden

ABOUT THE SELECTION

The Tewas are one of the Pueblo peoples who live in the American Southwest. Although Spanish explorers entered their territory in the 1500s, the Pueblos have resisted outside influences and have retained many of their customs to the present day. "Song of the Sky Loom" was translated and published for English-speaking readers in 1933.

Oh our Mother the Earth, oh our Father the Sky,
Your children are we, and with tired backs
We bring you the gifts that you love.

Then weave for us a garment of brightness;
May the warp[1] be the white light of morning,
May the weft[2] be the red light of evening,
May the fringes be the falling rain,
May the border be the standing rainbow.

Thus weave for us a garment of brightness
That we may walk fittingly where birds sing,
That we may walk fittingly where grass is green,

Oh our Mother the Earth, oh our Father the Sky!

---

[1] threads that run lengthwise in a woven fabric

[2] horizontal threads interlaced through the warp in a woven fabric

When I Hear Your Name

by Gloria Fuertes

translated from Spanish by Ada Long and Philip Levine

ABOUT THE SELECTION

Gloria Fuertes is a major Spanish poet of the 20th century. The American poet David Ignatow has said that "Her voice in its anger and sadness is like nothing else among Spanish poets." Only a small amount of her poetry has been translated into English, in a volume called *Off the Map: Selected Poems by Gloria Fuertes.* "When I Hear Your Name" is from that volume. If you are alert to the numbers in the poem, you may notice that it refers to an alphabet of 28 rather than 26 letters. That is because the Spanish alphabet has 24 letters in common with English—all but k and w—and 4 additional letter combinations that are counted as letters: *ch, ll, ñ, and rr.*

When I hear your name
I feel a little robbed of it;
it seems unbelievable
that half a dozen letters could say so much.

My compulsion[1] is to blast down every wall with
your name,
I'd paint it on all the houses,
there wouldn't be a well
I hadn't leaned into
to shout your name there,
nor a stone mountain
where I hadn't uttered
those six separate letters
that are echoed back.

[1] irresistible impulse to act, regardless of the sanity of the action or its reasons

My compulsion is
to teach the birds to sing it,
to teach the fish to drink it,
to teach men that there is nothing
like the madness of repeating your name.

My compulsion is to forget altogether
the other 22 letters, all the numbers,
the books I've read, the poems I've written.
To say hello with your name.
To beg bread with your name.
"She always says the same thing," they'd say
when they saw me,
and I'd be so proud, so happy, so self-contained.

And I'll go to the other world with your name on
my tongue,
and all their questions I'll answer with your
name
—judges and saints will understand nothing—
God will sentence me to repeating it endlessly
and forever.

Death, Be Not Proud

by John Donne

ABOUT THE SELECTION

John Donne (pronounced *dun*), born in 1572 in London, was one of England's most famous preachers at his death in 1631 and is now regarded as one of the major poets of his era. Only a few of his nearly 200 poems were published during his lifetime, but many were widely circulated in manuscript form. His writing is noted for its unexpected comparisons and unusual combinations of logic and emotion. Born a Catholic, Donne converted to Anglicanism (the state religion of England) in the 1590s and became secretary to a government official. When he secretly married the official's daughter, however, he lost his job. Patrons who enjoyed his poetry helped him and his family survive until he became an Anglican minister in 1615. He served as dean of St. Paul's Cathedral from 1621 until his death and often preached at court. In his later years his poems concerned religious themes. As "Death Be Not Proud" indicates, however, Donne continued to make startling and forceful combinations of words and images.

Death, be not proud, though some have called thee
Mighty and dreadful, for thou art not so;
For those whom thou think'st thou dost overthrow
Die not, poor Death, nor yet canst thou kill me.
From rest and sleep, which but thy pictures be,
Much pleasure; then from thee much more must flow,
And soonest our best men with thee do go,
Rest of their bones, and soul's delivery.
Thou art slave to fate, chance, kings, and desperate men,
And dost with poison, war, and sickness dwell;
And poppy or charms can make us sleep as well
And better than thy stroke; why swell'st thou then?
One short sleep past, we wake eternally,
And death shall be no more; Death, thou shalt die.

March 1st

by Kathleen Spivack

ABOUT THE SELECTION

Kathleen Spivack (1938–) is both a poet and a teacher of poetry who has contributed to many magazines and anthologies. She lives in Boston. In "March 1st," she compares features of the great outdoors to laundry found inside a Bendix-brand clothes dryer.

Coming out of the house on a fresh March morning,
I saw February still meandering around
like laundry caught in a Bendix. Stray shreds
of cloud, like pillow slips, were rent[1] from
her large endlessness. Outdated,
her decrepit[2] body garlanded itself disgracefully
with powder. She luxuriated in old age.
Even her graying sheets were still there,
tattered, heaped carelessly on the street,
bearing the indentation of someone's huge body
and furred with a fine fringe of soot.
She had been plump, she had been heavy, sitting
on top of us since January. Winter, you
old clothes hamper, what mildew
still molders inside you before March
dribbles a bit, dries up, and is done for?

---

[1] torn

[2] weakened, worn out, or broken down by old age or overuse

Birthday

by M. T. Buckley

ABOUT THE SELECTION

During World War II a famous unit of the U.S. infantry was the 82nd Airborne, whose members parachuted into battles. They were said to jump from their planes yelling, "Geronimo!" The poem "Birthday" begins with this cry. Into what battle does M. T. Buckley's speaker jump?

Geronimo.
I jumped into the world.
No parachute. Bootless,
falling into enemy territory
into the night (had my eyes closed).
Didn't take them long to find me.
These suicide missions are all the same.
Name? not yet. Unit? 82nd Newborn, ha ha.
Slapped me around a bit
but I didn't talk.
Made sure I wouldn't escape.
Sentenced me to life. I guess I deserved it.

Tiburón

by Martín Espada

ABOUT THE SELECTION

Martín Espada (1957–) was born in Brooklyn, New York, but his family moved to a suburb on Long Island when he was 13 years old. There, because of his Puerto Rican descent, he was an outsider, so he turned to writing poetry to express himself. He has now written four books of poetry and has become a teacher of creative writing. “Tiburón” calls on his Hispanic background in its mention of salsa music and in its title, which means “shark.”

East 116th
and a long red car
stalled with the hood up
roaring salsa
like a prize shark
mouth yanked open
and down in the stomach
the radio
of the last fisherman
still tuned
to his lucky station

Fall, leaves, fall

by Emily Brontë

ABOUT THE SELECTION

Emily Brontë (1818–1848), who lived most of her life in the family home on a lonely English moor, was both a poet and novelist. She became famous for her romantic tale of uncontrolled passion, *Wuthering Heights.* Her sisters Charlotte and Anne were also writers; all three contributed poems to their first published book, a volume of poetry. For more about Brontë's life, see About This Poet at the beginning of this unit. The poem below, "Fall, leaves, fall," suggests the poet's inclination toward strong and unconventional emotion.

Fall, leaves, fall; die, flowers, away;
Lengthen night and shorten day;
Every leaf speaks bliss to me
Fluttering from the autumn tree.
I shall smile when wreaths of snow
Blossom where the rose should grow;
I shall sing when night's decay
Ushers in a drearier day.

UNDERSTANDING THE POEMS

Record your answers to these questions in your personal literature notebook. Follow the directions for each group.

GROUP 1

Reread the poems in Group 1 to complete these sentences.

Reviewing the Selection

1. In "When I Hear Your Name" the only action that the speaker does not think of taking is
  a. teaching the birds to sing her lover's name.
  b. painting her lover's name on houses.
  c. branding her lover's name into gates and fences.
  d. saying hello with her lover's name.

2. "Song of the Sky Loom" asks for clothing made of
  a. light.
  b. earth and sky.
  c. evening.
  d. grass.

Interpreting the Selection

3. In saying that Death is "slave to fate, chance, kings, and desperate men," the speaker of "Death, Be Not Proud" means that
  a. the slaves of kings would rather be dead.
  b. accidents and violent people cause deaths, and so control death.
  c. some lucky people, such as kings, can choose when to die.
  d. kings are desperate men who have slaves.

Recognizing How Words Are Used

4. In "The Waning Moon" a mood of depression is suggested by the words and phrases
  a. *lean and pale, gauzy veil,* and *arose.*
  b. *dying lady, totters,* and *insane and feeble wanderings.*
  c. *lady, out of her chamber,* and *East.*
  d. *wrapped in a gauzy veil, led,* and *the moon arose.*

Appreciating Poetry

5. When the writer of "Metaphor" says that night files away what you say, she means that
a. talking is the same as writing.
b. what is said and done cannot be changed later.
c. you should put away your writing every evening.
d. every night you dream about what you said during the day.

GROUP 2 Reread the poems in Group 2 to complete these sentences.

Reviewing the Selection

6. In "Tiburón" the speaker imagines a shark that has swallowed
a. a car.
b. some salsa.
c. a radio.
d. water.

7. The favorite season of the speaker in "Fall, leaves, fall" is
a. spring.
b. summer.
c. fall.
d. winter.

Interpreting the Selection

8. When the speaker in "March 1st" discusses "graying sheets," she or he actually is referring to
a. dirty snow.
b. an old clothes hamper.
c. sheets of old newspapers.
d. gray skies.

Recognizing How Words Are Used

9. "Birthday" presents a unique view of
a. birth.
b. death.
c. war.
d. dangerous sports.

Appreciating Poetry

10. The tone of “Birthday” suggests a speaker who is
  a. a confused but optimistic child.
  b. a battle-weary and frightened soldier.
  c. a remorseful criminal sentenced for wrongdoing.
  d. the cocky, know-it-all hero in a war movie.

Now check your answers with your teacher. Study the questions you answered incorrectly. What types of questions were they? Talk with your teacher about ways to work on those skills.

Figurative Language

We are forever making comparisons. Proof of that is in our vocabulary and expressions. For example, we "bounce" ideas off other people, get caught up in the "rat race," and feel "happy as a lark" when we're successful. We use comparisons so often that we don't even notice what we're saying when we use them. Such overused comparisons, or *clichés*, would be useless in poems. No poet wants to recycle old comparisons that won't demand the attention of readers. Instead, to lead readers to think creatively, poets search for new comparisons. They try to bring together two unlike things in such a way that readers are forced to think about common things in uncommon ways. Making such comparisons is known as using *figurative language*, or *figures of speech*.

Metaphors, similes, and other comparisons are all examples of figurative language. This unit will discuss the following characteristics of figurative language:

1. Poets can use effective metaphors, similes, or other figures of speech to help readers discover unexpected similarities between two people or objects.

2. Figures of speech evoke in readers particular ideas and feelings, enabling the poet to express themes more powerfully than would otherwise be possible.

LESSON 1 FIGURES OF SPEECH

All types of figurative language have one common goal—to make readers think of objects or experiences as if they were something different. In the process, readers discover things about the objects or experiences that are not normally seen or considered. We can separate figures of speech into several categories, including *simile*, several types of *metaphor*, *personification*, and *hyperbole*.

A *simile* is a direct comparison between two unlike things, which uses the word *like* or *as* or the verb *appears* or *seems*. The entire poem "The Waning Moon" is a single simile. The two items being compared are the moon and a dying lady:

> And like a dying lady, lean and pale,
> Who totters forth, wrapped in a gauzy veil, . . .
> The moon arose up in the murky East,
> A white and shapeless mass.

A *metaphor* is an implied comparison between two unlike things. Without using *like*, *as*, *appears*, or *seems*, a metaphor suggests that one thing *is* another. Notice how the title of "Song of the Sky Loom" calls the sky a loom. The poem then goes into detail about how the sky acts as a loom. By identifying forces of nature with the threads and parts of clothing, the metaphor stresses the connection between humans and nature:

> Then weave for us a garment of brightness;
> May the warp be the white light of morning,
> May the weft be the red light of evening,
> May the fringes be the falling rain,
> May the border be the standing rainbow.

The metaphor of the sky loom is not merely stated and then forgotten; it is developed throughout the entire poem. This is an example of an *extended metaphor*.

Another type of metaphor is an *implied metaphor*. In this type of metaphor, one of the things in the comparison is not named; its identity is simply suggested. For example, in the lines of "The Waning Moon" quoted earlier, where the poet states that the moon looks like a dying lady, he does not state that the clouds are her veil. However, the comparison is strongly suggested.

Writers use *personification* to give human qualities to an

object, animal, or idea. In "Song of the Sky Loom," for example, the speaker addresses the earth and sky as people:

> Oh our Mother the Earth, oh our Father the Sky,
> Your children are we, . . .

A stronger example of personification, however, is found in "Death, Be Not Proud." Here, the speaker not only talks directly to an event as if it were a listening person, that event is also given the human characteristics of pride, might, and faulty thinking:

> Death, be not proud, though some have called thee
> Mighty and dreadful, for thou art not so;
> For those whom thou think'st thou dost overthrow
> Die not, poor Death, nor yet canst thou kill me.

Hyperbole is an exaggeration that is made to emphasize a point. All of the poem "When I Hear Your Name" consists of hyperbole intended to show how the speaker feels about his or her loved one's name—and the loved one as well.

> My compulsion is to blast down every wall with
>   your name,
> I'd paint it on all the houses,
> there wouldn't be a well
> I hadn't leaned into
> to shout your name there, . . .
>
> My compulsion is
> to teach the birds to sing it,
> to teach the fish to drink it, . . .
>
> God will sentence me to repeating it endlessly
>   and forever.

EXERCISE 1

Reread the poems in Group 1. Then use what you have learned in this lesson to answer these questions:

1. What two things are compared in the central metaphor in "Metaphor"? What likeness(es) does the poet point out?
2. In "Death, Be Not Proud" what does the speaker say are "pictures" of death? Explain the similarities.

Now check your answers with your teacher. Review this part of the lesson if you don't understand why an answer was incorrect.

WRITING ON YOUR OWN 

In this lesson you studied four types of figurative language. Of the four, simile and metaphor are used most often. In this exercise you will write original similes and metaphors. Follow these steps:

- Review the notes that you wrote for the introductory writing exercise. Choose two of the topics on your lists. You will write at least one simile and one metaphor about each topic.
- Reflect on one of the topics you selected and write words or phrases to describe it. For example, if you chose a "lucky" shirt, you might describe its appearance and some of the positive experiences you have had while wearing it.
- So far, your details about your first topic have been concrete and realistic. Now consider comparisons that suggest abstract or unusual similarities. For example, you might think of your lucky shirt as a wizard's cape, or you might recall that you wore it while effortlessly climbing a hill that seemed as high as Mt. Everest. Write at least one simile and one metaphor that express your attitude toward your chosen topic.

- Now reflect on your second topic and repeat the same procedure. Write at least one simile and one metaphor that express your attitude toward your second topic.
- Save your figures of speech and your lists of possible topics to use in later writing exercises.

LESSON 2 HOW FIGURATIVE LANGUAGE EXPRESSES THEME

Imagine that you go to a party and you have a wonderful time. The next time you see a friend who wasn't there, you try to share your experiences with him or her. You tell your friend who else was at the party, what they said, and what they did. The more you talk, however, the more bored your friend looks. Your words simply can't capture all the fun that you had. After a while you give up and say, "You had to be there to understand."

Reading a good figure of speech is very much like attending that party. You can restate at least some of its original meaning after you've read it, but by not using its exact words you lose its freshness and emotional impact. Just as the party would not have been the same with a different mix of guests, removing or replacing a figure of speech changes a poem.

Look, for example, at the simile that is the core of "Tiburón":

> and a long red car
> stalled with the hood up . . .
>
> like a prize shark
> mouth yanked open

The poet is pointing out that this particular car looks like a powerful and dangerous creature, capable of destroying those who try to tame it. The very fact that he thought of this simile, and that we see something fitting in it, suggests a more general theme: Our machinery can take on a life and power of its own and can sometimes pose a danger to us. This restatement—

because it is a restatement—overstates what the poem expresses. Much of the power of the poem comes from the ease with which we identify the car with a fearful shark.

The figurative language in "March 1st" is somewhat less precise: February is pictured as both an old woman and dirty laundry. To try to explain how these two images work together would ruin the poem. But the details of the figures of speech build the mood of frustration we all feel after a long, dreary spell of gray clouds and old snow that resists melting:

> Even her graying sheets were still there,
> tattered, heaped carelessly on the street,
> bearing the indentation of someone's huge body
> and furred with a fine fringe of soot.
> She had been plump, she had been heavy, sitting
> on top of us since January.

The poem ends with an *apostrophe* (the technique of addressing a thing or an absent person) to Winter that evokes a feeling of repulsion toward the late-winter weather:

> Winter, you
> old clothes hamper, what mildew
> still molders inside you before March
> dribbles a bit, dries up, and is done for?

EXERCISE 2

Reread the poems in Group 2. Then use what you have learned in this lesson to answer these questions:

1. Discuss how the identity of the speaker depends on the extended metaphor in "Birthday." Identify both the metaphor and the speaker. What is the speaker's tone, or attitude, toward his situation? What theme do you believe the metaphor and speaker express?

2. Identify an instance of each of these figures of speech in "Fall, leaves, fall": metaphor, personification, apostrophe. How do these figures of speech enable the poem to demand attention and make its theme of "Misery loves company" sound fresh?

Now check your answers with your teacher. Review this part of the lesson if you don't understand why an answer was incorrect.

WRITING ON YOUR OWN 

In Writing on Your Own 1 you wrote both similes and metaphors. For this exercise you will develop an example of either personification or hyperbole. Follow these steps:

- Decide whether you will work with personification or hyperbole. Then review the list of possible topics that you created earlier. Choose a topic that you think lends itself to your technique. Then, as you did for Writing on Your Own 1, reflect on the topic you chose and write phrases that describe it and your experiences with it.
- If you are working with personification and your topic is a thing or idea, can you personify the topic? What do the details on your list suggest about the characteristics of the "person" that the topic should become? If your topic is already a person, find an object or quality in the details that can be personified. For example, a person's habit of strict attention to detail might be personified as a police officer, a drill sergeant, or a judge. Write at least three lines that develop your example of personification. Your lines need not rhyme or have regular rhythm.
- If you are working with hyperbole, focus on a characteristic or a feeling that can be exaggerated in such a way as to show the extent of your feelings or attitude. For example, if the speaker of your poem is a little boy, you may want to suggest

that he sees a particular adult as a giant. Or if the speaker is you and you are trying to decide what to do after high school, you may say that you think about it every minute of every day. Write at least three lines to present your hyperbole. Your lines need not rhyme or have regular rhythm.

- Save your new figure of speech and your previous writing assignments to use at the end of this unit.

DISCUSSION GUIDES

1. The nine poems in this unit were chosen because they provide vivid illustrations of various figures of speech. What similarities do you find among them? Sort the poems into no more than four groups. If necessary, you may drop one of the poems. For each of your groups, write a brief explanation as to why you combined them as you did. Then compare your groups with those of others in the class. Did several people come up with the same groupings? Did they have the same reasons?

2. "March 1st" paints an unattractive picture of February, representing it as dirty laundry. Clearly, February must be that poet's least favorite month. What is your least favorite month? Why? With your class, list the disadvantages of each month. Then, together, choose an image (other than dirty laundry) to represent the worst quality of each month.

3. Choose a poem from this unit to present before classmates. Memorize it and practice presenting it with expression. Then perform the poem for your class.

WRITE A POEM WITH FIGURATIVE LANGUAGE

In this unit you have created several figures of speech. Now you will use figurative language to write a poem about a topic of personal importance.

Follow these steps to write your poem. If you have questions about the writing process, refer to Using the Writing Process on page 245.

- Assemble and review the work you did for all the writing exercises in this unit: 1) lists of ideas, people, things, and events about which you feel strongly; 2) similes and metaphors about two of those topics; 3) an example of either personification or hyperbole.
- Choose one of your listed topics to be the subject of your poem. If you'd like, use one of the topics about which you have already written. Decide what you want to describe and express in a poem that is at least eight lines long. Decide, also, whether your poem will be in free verse or a traditional, rhymed form.
- Your poem must include two or more instances of figurative language. These can include figures of speech from the Writing on Your Own exercises, if you'd like. Remember, also, to use alliteration, assonance, and/or consonance to give interest to your words. Write your poem.
- When you are finished, ask a classmate to read your poem aloud. Invite him or her to identify your figures of speech and to give his or her opinion of how well they expresses your meaning. If necessary, revise your poem and repeat this step until you are satisfied with your writing.
- Finally, proofread your poem for grammar and spelling errors. Then make a final copy of it and save it in your writing portfolio.

Form in Poetry

Oh Mistress Mine
by William Shakespeare

Stanzas
(When a Man Hath No Freedom to Fight for at Home)
by George Gordon Byron, 6th Baron Byron

Keeping Things Whole
by Mark Strand

She Walks in Beauty
by George Gordon Byron, 6th Baron Byron

The Eagle
by Alfred, Lord Tennyson

Villanelle VI
by Judith Barrington

Two Hokku Poems
by Richard Wright

If Thou Must Love Me, Let It Be for Naught
by Elizabeth Barrett Browning

Swan and Shadow
by John Hollander

INTRODUCTION

ABOUT THE LESSONS

When you sit down to write a letter, you know that you'll be using sentences that are organized in paragraphs. Each sentence will be as long as you choose to make it, and each paragraph will have as many sentences as it needs to make its point.

When writing some types of poetry, poets use the same approach, putting as many words in a line and as many lines in a stanza as they wish. Over the hundreds of years that poets have been writing in English, however, they have developed certain types of poems that follow much stricter forms. Each of these forms has a specific number of lines and stanzas and often follows a set rhythmic pattern and rhyme scheme. In this unit you will learn about some of these traditional forms of poetry.

WRITING: USING FORM IN A POEM

This unit discusses several traditional forms of poetry. Throughout the unit you will work with one or more classmates to write poems in three of those forms. Follow these steps to get started:

- Make a list of a half-dozen popular sports. You need not be a player or even a great fan of each sport, but you should at least know the terms associated with it. As you list each sport, indicate your level of knowledge and interest.
- Find other people in your class who have listed some of the same sports that you did. Write down each person's name and the sport or sports you listed in common. If the person's level of knowledge about each sport makes a difference to you, note that next to his or her name. When you collaborate for the writing exercises later on in this unit, you may choose new partners each time, so find more than one person with the same sports as yours.

ABOUT THIS POET

Richard Wright (1908–1960) was the first African American writer to achieve major acclaim and has been called one of the most important writers of the 20th century. He was a novelist, a short-story writer, an essayist, and a poet. Born in the South, he took an outspoken stand against racism as he described the effects of racial injustice on his characters. He powerfully expressed the rage that many blacks felt toward the society that excluded and oppressed them.

Wright was born on a farm near Natchez, Mississippi, and was mostly self-educated. He began writing after he moved to Chicago in 1927 and was hired by the Federal Writers' Project. He also became interested in communism and joined the Communist Party in 1932. In 1937 he moved to New York, where he became Harlem editor of the Communist newspaper *Daily Worker*. He left the party in 1944 and later explained his decision in an essay in *The God That Failed* (1949), his collection of writings by former Communists. After living in Mexico for a few years, he moved to France in 1946 and lived in Paris until he died.

Wright's first published work was *Uncle Tom's Children* (1938), a collection of four short novels about victims of racial injustice in the South. His first full-length novel was *Native Son* (1940), which is now considered a classic. It tells of a young black man in Chicago who, because of circumstances caused by racial prejudice, accidentally commits murder and is sentenced to death. Wright adapted the novel to the stage in 1941. It was also made into a movie twice.

Other works by Wright include *Black Boy* (1944), an account of his childhood and youth, regarded by many as his most important work; *White Man, Listen!* (1957), a collection of his essays; and *This Other World*, an unpublished collection of 800 haiku, a form also known as hokku.

AS YOU READ

As you read each poem in this unit, ask yourself these questions:

- Does this poem contain patterns of rhythm and rhyme? If it does, how can I describe them?
- Does this poem have characteristics that qualify it as a specific type? If so, what type of poem is it?
- How is this poem like or unlike other poems?

Oh Mistress Mine

by William Shakespeare

ABOUT THE SELECTION

William Shakespeare (1564–1616) is widely considered the greatest playwright of all time and the finest poet to use the English language. He was born in Stratford-upon-Avon in England and was educated in grammar schools there. He became an actor and a playwright in London and a member of a popular company of actors that often performed for royalty. Around 1608 Shakespeare moved back to Stratford and traveled back and forth from there to London until he died. He is best known for his plays, which include comedies, tragedies, and histories and are generally written in blank verse, a form of unrhymed poetry. The poem "Oh Mistress Mine" is a lighthearted song from his comedy *Twelfth Night.*

Oh mistress mine! where are you roaming?
Oh! stay and hear; your true love's coming,
        That can sing both high and low.
Trip no further, pretty sweeting;
Journeys end in lovers meeting,
        Every wise man's son doth know.

What is love? 'tis not hereafter;
Present mirth hath present laughter;
        What's to come is still unsure:
In delay there lies no plenty;
Then come kiss me, sweet and twenty,
        Youth's a stuff will not endure.

Stanzas

(When a Man Hath No Freedom to Fight for at Home)

by George Gordon Byron, 6th Baron Byron

ABOUT THE SELECTION

George Gordon Byron (1788–1824) was a freedom-loving English poet whose work and life created the "Byronic hero," a melancholy but self-confident and defiant man. At the age of 10, Byron inherited the title Lord Byron. He attended Cambridge University, served briefly in the House of Lords, and then traveled in Europe and the Near East. The long poem he wrote about his travels, the first two sections of *Childe Harold's Pilgrimage,* made him instantly famous in 1812. In 1816 he left England for Italy, where he became involved in Italian politics, supporting the nationalist movement. When that movement collapsed he went to Greece to take part in its fight for independence from Turkey. He died of a fever while in Greece.

At the time of his death Byron was working on his masterpiece, *Don Juan,* a comic epic poem. The ironic tone of "Stanzas" suggests Byron's wit and daring, as the poem reveals his awareness of the risks he was taking despite the small likelihood of its being appreciated.

When a man hath no freedom to fight for at home,
    Let him combat for that of his neighbors;
Let him think of the glories of Greece and of Rome,
    And get knocked on his head for his labors.

To do good to mankind is the chivalrous[1] plan,
    And is always as nobly requited;[2]
Then battle for freedom wherever you can,
    And, if not shot or hanged, you'll get knighted.[3]

---

[1] having the qualities of gallantry and honor associated with the ideal knight

[2] repaid

[3] honored by the (British) government by being named a knight

Keeping Things Whole

by Mark Strand

ABOUT THE SELECTION

Mark Strand (1934–) was born in Canada but was raised in the United States. He graduated from Antioch College and attended both the Yale Art School and the Iowa Writers Workshop. In 1990 he was named the fourth poet laureate of the United States. He is now professor of English at the University of Utah and a guest teacher at many other universities. Much of his poetry has been described as "surreal"—that is, dreamlike and bizarre, having unexpected arrangements of images. What images come to your mind as you read "Keeping Things Whole"?

In a field
I am the absence
of field.
This is
always the case.
Wherever I am
I am what is missing.

When I walk
I part the air
and always
the air moves in
to fill the spaces
where my body's been.
We all have reasons
for moving.
I move
to keep things whole.

She Walks in Beauty

by George Gordon Byron, 6th Baron Byron

ABOUT THE SELECTION "She Walks in Beauty" is probably Lord Byron's most famous short poem. In this classic, the speaker's tone is one of sincere admiration.

She walks in beauty, like the night
Of cloudless climes[1] and starry skies;
And all that's best of dark and bright
Meet in her aspect[2] and her eyes:
Thus mellowed to that tender light
Which heaven to gaudy day denies.

One shade the more, one ray the less,
Had half impaired[3] the nameless grace
Which waves in every raven tress,
Or softly lightens o'er her face;
Where thoughts serenely sweet express
How pure, how dear their dwelling-place.

And on that cheek, and o'er that brow,
So soft, so calm, yet eloquent,
The smiles that win, the tints that glow,
But tell of days in goodness spent,
A mind at peace with all below,
A heart whose love is innocent!

---

[1] weather

[2] facial expression

[3] caused to diminish or lessen, as in value

The Eagle

by Alfred, Lord Tennyson

ABOUT THE SELECTION

Alfred, Lord Tennyson (1809–1892) served as England's esteemed poet laureate from 1850 until his death. The son of a clergyman, Tennyson entered Cambridge University in 1828 and published his first book of poetry in 1830. His poems quickly became popular, but he lived quietly, devoting himself to his writing. He is known for his lyric poems, dramatic monologues, and long narratives. Two of his most important long works are *In Memoriam*, a collection of 133 poems in memory of his college friend Arthur Hallam, and *The Idylls of the King,* a series of 12 poems telling the tale of King Arthur. The poem below is a fragment written in 1851, intended for a longer work.

He clasps the crag with crooked hands;
Close to the sun in lonely lands,
Ringed with the azure[1] world, he stands.

The wrinkled sea beneath him crawls;
He watches from his mountain walls,
And like a thunderbolt he falls.

---

[1] light purplish-blue

Villanelle VI

by Judith Barrington

ABOUT THE SELECTION

Judith Barrington has had two collections of her poetry published—*Trying to Be an Honest Woman* and *History and Geography,* a finalist for the Oregon Book Award. In addition, she has edited a book about poets and has written the libretto for an oratorio (the words for a long musical composition). After her mother died by drowning, Barrington wrote a sequence of six villanelles about the event. She explained why she chose the villanelle form: "I do not think I could have written that particular piece without a strict form. The boundaries—the finite patterns that could not spill out into the unknown—provided a framework that I needed for the subject. . . . I had always thought that the shape of the villanelle, with its repeating lines that come together at the end, suggested both tides and circles. These poems were full of ocean, waves and moon." Here is the sixth poem of that sequence.

When I stand on the shore, I wonder where you are
somewhere in that fathomed room behind
the waves like doors that slowly swing ajar.

Dappled stones at my feet are smeared with tar.
Sucked by the undertow, they jostle and grind
while I stand on the shore, wondering where you are.

Beyond the raging surf, beyond the bar,
in your green chamber you hide, forever blind
to the waves like doors that slowly swing ajar

inviting me in, enticing me from afar,
but their curling crests are an unmistakable sign
I should stay on shore and wonder where you are.

Your voice in the wind doesn't say where you are
and I listen less and less, resigned
to those waves like doors that slowly swing ajar.

Will the light of the crescent moon, the northern star
create a pathway we both can find
as I stand on the shore wondering where you are,
and the waves like doors slowly swing ajar?

Two Hokku Poems

by Richard Wright

ABOUT THE SELECTION

Richard Wright (1908–1960) was one of the most influential African American writers of the 20th century. Born in the South, he wrote primarily about the violence and rage caused by racial injustice. To escape discrimination in America, Wright moved to France in 1946. While there he became interested in hokku, or haiku. He wrote about 4,000 poems in this form and selected 800 of them for publication. The collection, *This Other World*, has not been published in its entirety, but about two dozen of Wright's hokku have appeared in articles and biographies. Below are two of them. For more information about Wright, see About This Poet at the beginning of this unit.

The spring lingers on
In the scent of a damp log
Rotting in the sun

The crow flew so fast
That he left his lonely caw
Behind in the fields

If Thou Must Love Me, Let It Be for Naught

by Elizabeth Barrett Browning

ABOUT THE SELECTION

Elizabeth Barrett Browning (1806–1861) was a famous poet of the Victorian era who is now best known for the poems she wrote to her husband, poet Robert Browning. She was well-educated at home by her domineering father. Her health was poor, so after her family moved to London she stayed in a dark room, reading and writing. Robert Browning liked her *Poems* (1844) so much, however, that he began visiting her. The two fell in love, married secretly in 1846, and soon after ran off to Italy. There her health improved greatly, and she had a son in 1849. The selection below is one of her *Sonnets from the Portuguese* (1850), her collection of love poems to her husband.

If thou must love me, let it be for naught
Except for love's sake only. Do not say,
"I love her for her smile—her look—her way
Of speaking gently—for a trick of thought
That falls in well with mine, and certes[1] brought
A sense of pleasant ease on such a day"—
For these things in themselves, Belovèd, may
Be changed, or change for thee—and love, so wrought,[2]
May be unwrought so. Neither love me for
Thine own dear pity's wiping my cheeks dry—
A creature might forget to weep, who bore
Thy comfort long, and lose thy love thereby!
But love me for love's sake, that evermore
Thou may'st love on, through love's eternity.

---

[1] certainly

[2] made

Swan and Shadow

by John Hollander

ABOUT THE SELECTION

Poet and professor John Hollander (1929–) was born in New York City. He earned degrees at Columbia and Indiana University and published his first book of poetry in 1958. He is now professor of English at Yale. In 1983 he won the Bollingen Prize for poetry. As you read this unusually shaped poem, read continuously from left to right without stopping between words on the lines that are broken by the spaces in the image.

Dusk
Above the
water hang the
loud
flies
Here
O so
gray
then
What A pale signal will appear
When Soon before its shadow fades
Where Here in this pool of opened eye
In us No Upon us As at the very edges
of where we take shape in the dark air
this object bares its image awakening
ripples of recognition that will
brush darkness up into light
even after this bird this hour both drift by atop the perfect sad instant now
already passing out of sight
toward yet-untroubled reflection
this image bears its object darkening
into memorial shades Scattered bits of
light No of water Or something across
water Breaking up No Being regathered
soon Yet by then a swan will have
gone Yes out of mind into what
vast
pale
hush
of a
place
past
sudden dark as
if a swan
sang

UNDERSTANDING THE POEMS

Record your answers to these questions in your personal literature notebook. Follow the directions for each group.

GROUP 1

Reread the poems in Group 1 to complete these sentences.

Reviewing the Selection

1. In "Keeping Things Whole" the speaker calls himself or herself
   a. a field.
   b. the absence of field.
   c. the case.
   d. the air.

Interpreting the Selection

2. The speaker in "Stanzas (When a Man Hath No Freedom to Fight for at Home)" advises others to
   a. fight for freedom wherever it is needed.
   b. mind their own business.
   c. get knocked on the head.
   d. fight with their neighbors.

3. The theme of "Oh Mistress Mine" can best be restated as
   a. "He who laughs last laughs best."
   b. "Good things come to those who wait."
   c. "The longest journey begins with one step."
   d. "Enjoy the moment; don't wait for tomorrow."

Recognizing How Words Are Used

4. In the lines "She walks in Beauty, like the night/Of cloudless climes and starry skies;" the poet used the word *climes* instead of *weather* for all these reasons *except* that
   a. *climes* is harder to understand than *weather.*
   b. *climes* has only one syllable, while *weather* has two.
   c. the vowel sound of *climes* is long *i.*
   d. *cloudless* and *climes* both begin with *cl.*

Appreciating Poetry

5. In "The Eagle" the attitude of the speaker toward the eagle is one of
  a. indifference.
  b. pity.
  c. jealousy.
  d. awe.

GROUP 2

Reread the poems in Group 2 to complete these sentences.

Reviewing the Selection

6. In the hokku about the log, we can be sure that
  a. the season is spring.
  b. the day is very hot.
  c. it is raining.
  d. the log is sitting in water.

7. The speaker in "Villanelle VI" is standing
  a. on a shore.
  b. in a "fathomed" room.
  c. in a green chamber.
  d. near doors that swing ajar.

Interpreting the Selection

8. In "Swan and Shadow" the speaker
  a. chases the swan away and later regrets it.
  b. tries to capture the swan.
  c. sees the swan for a moment as it floats away.
  d. believes that the swan is just a hallucination.

Recognizing How Words Are Used

9. The phrase *curling crests* in "Villanelle VI" is an example of
  a. simile.
  b. personification.
  c. alliteration.
  d. onomatopoeia.

Appreciating Poetry

10. In "If Thou Must Love Me, Let It Be for Naught" the speaker starts out by telling her beloved what he should not do. Then, however, she starts telling him what he *should* do in line
  a. three.
  b. seven.
  c. eleven.
  d. thirteen.

Now check your answers with your teacher. Study the questions you answered incorrectly. What types of questions were they? Talk with your teacher about ways to work on those skills.

Form in Poetry

Imagine that you have never owned or used a camera. To you, all cameras would seem pretty much the same: a box with a lens and a light. Imagine, however, that before a vacation you decided to get a decent camera to record your adventures. After a few visits to different camera departments and some research on what is available, you would look at cameras with new eyes. For the first time, you would see differences among them. You would have an idea of when a video camera would be more useful for your needs than a still camera, and vice versa. You would know whether to expect certain features on a particular class of camera and where to look for them. You wouldn't be an expert, but you would be able to discuss cameras intelligently.

Similarly, at this stage of your study of poetry you may see little difference between blank verse and free verse, between a couplet and a sonnet, and between an iamb and a trochee. By the end of this unit, however, you should be able to recognize some important characteristics of poetry and should know which characteristics to look for in some popular forms. You'll have the vocabulary to discuss these forms, not as an expert, but intelligently. The lessons in this unit will focus on these points:

1. The forms of poems are defined in terms of rhyme schemes and rhythmic patterns.
2. Some distinct forms of poetry are the haiku or hokku, the sonnet, the villanelle, and the concrete poem.

LESSON 1

RHYTHM AND RHYME

To discuss different forms of poetry, it is first necessary to understand terms relating to rhythm and rhyme. *Rhythm* is the pattern of stressed and unstressed syllables in a poem. *Rhyme* is the repetition of the same or similar vowel and consonant sounds at the ends of words.

Rhythm In Unit 4 you learned that poets can create regular patterns of stressed and unstressed syllables, or they can use conversational, irregular rhythms in their poems. You also learned that all rhythms, regular or irregular, are combinations of units of measure called *feet.* A *foot* consists of at least one stressed syllable and, usually, one or more unstressed syllables. There are five basic feet in English:

spondee—two stressed syllables, as in the word *childhood*

trochee—a stressed syllable followed by an unstressed syllable, as in *traffic*

dactyl—a stressed syllable followed by two unstressed syllables, as in *accident*

iamb—an unstressed syllable followed by a stressed syllable, as in *expect*

anapest—two unstressed syllables followed by a stressed syllable, as in *undisturbed*

Poetry written in the rhythms of normal conversation is called *free verse.* In free verse, as in conversation, all the patterns listed above are mixed together. See, for example, "Keeping Things Whole." Here the stressed and unstressed syllables in the first stanza of that poem are marked. Notice how the kinds and numbers of feet change from line to line:

∪ ∪ /
In a field
/ ∪ ∪ / ∪
I am the absence
∪ /
of field.
/ ∪
This is
/ ∪ ∪ /
always the case.
∪ / ∪ ∪ /
Wherever I am
∪ / ∪ ∪ / ∪
I am what is missing.

In a poem with a *meter,* or regular pattern, one foot is used over and over. The meter is defined by two things: the type of foot used and the number of feet in a line. Here is an example of *trochaic tetrameter,* that is, a pattern of four trochee feet in each line:

/ ∪ / ∪ / ∪ / ∪
Trip no further, pretty sweeting;
/ ∪ / ∪ / ∪ / ∪
Journeys end in lovers meeting,

If all lines of a poem kept strictly to a single meter, the poem would seem stiff and boring. Therefore, almost every poem includes variations on the chosen meter. Look for the rhythmic variations in the complete stanza of "Oh Mistress Mine," to which the preceding lines belong:

∪ / ∪ / ∪ / ∪ / ∪
Oh mistress mine! where are you roaming?
∪ / ∪ / ∪ / ∪ / ∪
Oh! stay and hear; your true love's coming,
/ ∪ / ∪ / ∪ /
That can sing both high and low.
/ ∪ / ∪ / ∪ / ∪
Trip no further, pretty sweeting;
/ ∪ / ∪ / ∪ / ∪
Journeys end in lovers meeting,
/ ∪ / ∪ / ∪ /
Every wise man's son doth know.

Variations in this stanza include an extra unstressed syllable at the beginning of lines 1 and 2 and the loss of the final unstressed syllable in lines 3 and 6. These are minor variations that don't interfere with the identification of this lyric's meter as trochaic tetrameter.

Besides *tetrameter,* other important metric terms are *monometer*—one foot per line; *dimeter*—two feet per line; *trimeter*—three feet per line; and *pentameter*—five feet per line.

One often-used meter is *iambic pentameter.* As you can determine from the name, this meter uses five iambic feet in each line. This rhythm sounds conversational but at the same time has a regular arrangement of stressed and unstressed syllables. Because iambic pentameter is so close to natural speech rhythms in English, it is one of the most popular meters, especially for longer poems. For example, Lord Byron's *Don Juan*—which was unfinished at the poet's death and has 222 stanzas in the first part alone—was written in rhymed iambic pentameter. Poems written in unrhymed iambic pentameter are said to be in *blank verse*. Aside from the songs and some passages that are not poetry, Shakespeare's plays are in blank verse.

Rhyme Schemes and Stanzas In Unit 4 you learned about different kinds of rhymes, such as masculine and feminine rhymes and internal and end rhymes. You also learned that to indicate a rhyme scheme you write a letter of the alphabet for each line of a stanza, repeating a single letter for every line that rhymes with the first line assigned that letter. For example, the rhyme scheme of the stanza from "Oh Mistress Mine" that was quoted earlier is *aabccb*. It is assigned these letters because lines 1 and 2 rhyme, lines 3 and 6 rhyme, and lines 4 and 5 rhyme.

Just as blank verse is defined by its meter, some forms of poetry are defined by their rhyme schemes. For example, a *couplet* is composed of two lines with end rhyme. A *tercet*, however, is composed of three lines that may or may not have end rhyme. The stanzas of "The Eagle" are tercets. Here is the first stanza, with its rhyme scheme marked:

He clasps the crag with crooked hands; *a*
Close to the sun in lonely lands, *a*
Ringed with the azure world, he stands. *a*

A *quatrain* is composed of four lines with such rhyme schemes as *abab, abba,* or others. Byron's "Stanzas (When a Man Hath No Freedom to Fight for at Home)" is composed of two quatrains. Here is the rhyme scheme of the first stanza:

When a man hath no freedom to fight for at home, *a*
Let him combat for that of his neighbors; *b*
Let him think of the glories of Greece and of Rome, *a*
And get knocked on his head for his labors. *b*

These simple stanza forms—couplet, tercet, and quatrain—are often used as building blocks for longer verse forms, such as the sonnet. As you read poems with more than four lines, you will notice that many of them are combinations of these short forms.

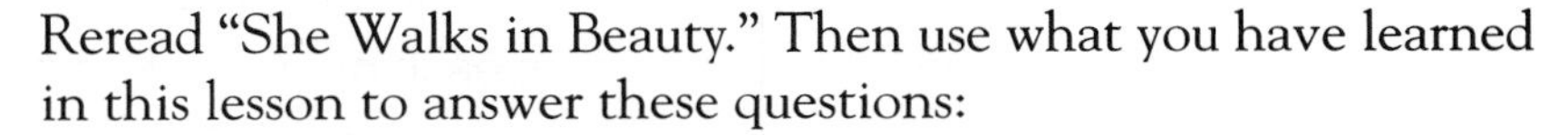

EXERCISE 1

Reread "She Walks in Beauty." Then use what you have learned in this lesson to answer these questions:

1. Copy the first stanza of "She Walks in Beauty," leaving a line of space above and below each line. Mark the stressed and unstressed syllables according to your judgment, keeping in mind that there will be some variations from a strict pattern. How many feet does each line have? What type of foot is used most often? Identify which of these meters is used in the poem: trochaic tetrameter, trochaic pentameter, iambic tetrameter, iambic pentameter.
2. How many lines are in each stanza? What rhyme scheme(s) do you find in the stanzas?

Now check your answers with your teacher. Review this part of the lesson if you don't understand why an answer was incorrect.

WRITING ON YOUR OWN 

In this lesson you learned about the basic rhythmic feet and short stanzaic forms. Now you will use what you learned to write two short poems about sports. Follow these steps:

- Find one or two partners whose lists have two sports in common with your list.
- With your partner or partners brainstorm a list of terms related to each sport. On each word of more than one syllable, mark the stressed and unstressed syllables. Decide which rhythmic pattern the word illustrates. Then evaluate the words, one list at a time. Does one rhythmic pattern show up more often than any other? If so, use that pattern in your poem about that sport. If the same rhythmic pattern shows up on both lists, choose a different pattern for your second poem. To decide on your second pattern, you may want to look at the words you are likely to use more than once in your poem.
- After you have chosen the rhythm you will use, choose a stanzaic form and a rhyme scheme for each poem. Use either a tercet or a quatrain for each of these short poems. The tercet may use an *aaa* or *aba* rhyme scheme or none at all. The quatrain may use an *abcb, abab,* or *abba* rhyme scheme.
- With your partner or partners write the two poems. Be careful to keep the rhythm regular, but pay attention to the meaning of the words as well. It should be clear from your poem what sport you are discussing, even if you don't use its name.
- Make copies of your poems so that each person has a set. Exchange poems with another writing team. Each team should be able to identify the rhythmic pattern, the stanzaic form, and the rhyme scheme of each of the other team's poems.

FOUR FORMS OF POETRY

If you tell someone that you are writing a poem in quatrains, all he or she would know is that each stanza in your poem is four lines long. If you were to say that your poem is a Shakespearean sonnet, however, that person probably could guess the line length, the rhyme scheme, and the organization of thoughts, since all these characteristics are defined by the form itself. In this lesson you will study the characteristics that define a haiku or hokku, a sonnet, a villanelle, and a concrete poem.

Haiku, or hokku *Haiku*, or *hokku*, is a form of poetry that is based on Japanese poetry. In a haiku the important sound pattern is the number of syllables. There should be a total of 17 syllables, divided among three lines in a 5–7–5 pattern. A haiku that follows Japanese tradition closely is also limited in its content. According to tradition the speaker should both observe nature and reflect on the scene observed. All the images and thoughts about them should occur at once.

Count the syllables in this hokku by Richard Wright. Does it have the correct number and pattern? Notice how the sensory image of the log's scent provokes the instant memory of spring, so that observation and reflection happen at the same time.

> The spring lingers on
> In the scent of a damp log
> Rotting in the sun

Sonnet A *sonnet* is a 14-line poem with a regular meter, which is most often iambic pentameter. Usually there is a development in thought over the course of the poem. First a situation or problem is described, and then there is a response to the situation or an answer to the problem.

In an Italian sonnet the first 8 lines, consisting of 2 quatrains, present the situation or problem. The last 6 lines present the response or answer. The rhyme scheme is usually *abba abba cdcdcd* or *abba abba cdecde*.

In a Shakespearean sonnet the first 12 lines consist of three quatrains and the last 2 lines are a rhymed couplet. The rhyme scheme is usually *abab cdcd efef gg*. Sometimes the thought break is between lines 8 and 9, but often the quatrains present the first thought and the couplet presents the response.

For an example of a sonnet in this unit, see "If Thou Must Love Me, Let It Be for Naught" on page 185.

Villanelle A *villanelle* is a 19-line poem composed of 5 tercets and a concluding quatrain. The first and third lines of the first stanza reappear alternately as the final line of the other tercets and then as the last 2 lines of the quatrain. Generally the middle line of every stanza rhymes. The rhyme scheme is usually *aba aba aba aba aba abaa*. Here are the first 3 stanzas of "Villanelle VI." Compare lines 1 and 3 of the first stanza with lines 1 and 3 of the next 2 stanzas.

> When I stand on the shore, I wonder where you are
> somewhere in that fathomed room behind
> the waves like doors that slowly swing ajar.
>
> Dappled stones at my feet are smeared with tar.
> Sucked by the undertow, they jostle and grind
> while I stand on the shore, wondering where you are.
>
> Beyond the raging surf, beyond the bar,
> in your green chamber you hide, forever blind
> to the waves like doors that slowly swing ajar

There are small differences in the repetition from stanza 1 to stanza 2: *When* becomes *while*, and *I wonder* becomes *wondering*. The line repeated in stanza 3 simply gains the word *to*. These slight changes contribute to the development of the thought from stanza to stanza. Note, for example, how lines 2-3 of stanza 1 describe a "fathomed room behind/the waves like doors . . . ." When the phrase about the waves reappears as line 3 of stanza 3, this stanza describes the person hidden in the fathomed room, who is "forever blind/to the waves like doors . . . ."

The villanelle is a very difficult form to use effectively. If you try your hand at one, you will discover that it's not easy to make the repeated lines bring out a new thought each time they reappear, in order to build to the message of the final quatrain. The challenge of the form, however, is one of the reasons poets like it.

Concrete poem Some poems take their form not from their sounds but from their appearance. Their shapes are related to their topics. Poems such as these are called *concrete poems*. "Swan and Shadow" is a particularly stunning example of a concrete poem in which the arrangement of the words reflects their content perfectly. Turn to page 187 to examine the image as a whole. In this excerpt notice how the spaces breaking the lines reinforce the question-and-answer nature of the words.

> What A pale signal will appear
> When Soon before its shadow fades
> Where Here in this pool of opened eye
> In us No Upon us As at the very edges
> of where we take shape in the dark air

EXERCISE 2

Reread the poems in Group 2. Then use what you have learned in this lesson to answer these questions:

1. In the second hokku by Wright, what object in nature is observed? What is the poet's thought, or reflection, concerning this object?
2. Study the poems "If Thou Must Love Me, Let It Be for Naught" and "Shall I Compare Thee to a Summer's Day?" (page 126). Decide if each poem is an Italian sonnet or a Shakespearean sonnet.
3. State the theme of "Villanelle VI" in your own words.

Now check your answers with your teacher. Review this part of the lesson if you don't understand why an answer was incorrect.

WRITING ON YOUR OWN 

In this lesson you studied, among other forms, the sonnet and the concrete poem. Now as part of a team you will write a poem in one of those forms. Follow these steps:

- Decide which sport you would like to write about and which form you would like to use. Then find one or more classmates who would like to work on the same type of poem.
- If you intend to write a sonnet, list words related to the sport and brainstorm several rhyming words for each word on your list. Then review the requirements of a sonnet as described in this lesson. Remember that the first part of a sonnet—either 8 or 12 lines—should present a situation or problem, and the second part—either 6 or 2 lines—should present a response or an answer. For example, the first part could describe the exciting final moments in a game, and the second part could describe the joy of the winners or the disappointment of the losers. Write your sonnet, satisfying the requirements for rhythm and rhyme.
- If you intend to write a concrete poem, decide what form your words will take. Then decide if the poem will use a regular rhythm and rhyme scheme or if it will be in free verse. Discuss what ideas your poem should convey. Finally, write your poem, arranging the words to create the image you chose. You may have to revise it a few times to get the words positioned just right.
- Make copies of your poem so that each group member has one. Exchange poems with another writing team that produced the same type of poem. After you read the other team's work, exchange comments on the poems. Remember to be helpful in your suggestions, not overly critical, and to be open-minded in your response to the other team's comments.

DISCUSSION GUIDES

1. Three poems in this unit are love poems: "Oh Mistress Mine," "She Walks in Beauty," and "If Thou Must Love Me, Let It Be for Naught." With a small group, compare and contrast these poems. Discuss these points and any others that group members raise: Do all three poems express the same kind of love and the same kind of relationship between lovers? If so, describe the relationship. If not, identify the differences. Which poem do you think is the sincerest expression of love? Which do you think is the most beautiful?

2. Do you agree with the opinions expressed in "Stanzas (When a Man Hath No Freedom to Fight for at Home)"? Are people truly unappreciative of the help given them by their neighboring countries? If Byron really believed what he said, why did he get involved in the Greek fight for independence? With a small group or the whole class, develop a short multiple-choice questionnaire that you would send to Byron if he were still alive, the answers to which would clarify his real feelings on the topic and his purpose for writing the poem.

3. With a partner or a small group, prepare "Villanelle VI" for presentation. Decide whether to assign lines to individual speakers or to a chorus. Decide whether the repeated lines will be given special handling. Practice reading the poem at the tempo you believe is best for developing the mood of the poem. Then present the poem to your class.

4. Research one of the poets in this unit. Present your findings in one of these forms: a time line, a chart, a newspaper obituary, a skit, a poster, or a poem.

USE FORM IN A POEM

In this unit you have studied some important forms of poetry. You have written poems in such forms as the tercet, quatrain, sonnet, and concrete poem. Now you will write a villanelle about a sport.

Follow these steps to write your villanelle. If you have questions about the writing process, refer to Using the Writing Process on page 245.

- Assemble and review the work you did for all the writing exercises in this unit: 1) a list of sports, 2) two poems on sports in tercet or quatrain form, 3) a sonnet or a concrete poem about a sport.
- Find one or more classmates interested in writing about the same sport. Reread the villanelle in this unit to remind yourselves of a typical line length and rhythm used in villanelles. Also review the explanation of a villanelle given on pages 197–198.
- Do some brainstorming to create a number of lines that could describe repeated events in the sport or reactions to the game. For example, you might come up with "As the ball flies up, the fans start to cheer" or "Run, run, before the clock runs out of time." Choose two of the lines you created to work with, making sure that each one ends in a word for which you can think of many other rhymes. Then write your first tercet, using your two chosen lines as lines 1 and 3.
- Create a skeleton outline for the rest of your poem, as indicated on page 203. Then discuss events or images that, combined with the existing lines, tell about the game. Fill in the missing lines so that the first line of every stanza rhymes with your repeated lines and each stanza makes sense. For this exercise you need not make the second line of every stanza rhyme. Try to make the rhythm regular, but that is less important than the rhyme scheme and thought.

(Tercet 1) line 1
line 2
line 3
(Tercet 2) ___
___
line 1
(Tercet 3) ___
___
line 3
(Tercet 4) ___
___
line 1
(Tercet 5) ___
___
line 3
(Quatrain) ___
___
line 1
line 3

- Exchange villanelles with another writing team, comment on each other's work, and make any revisions that you agree are needed. Then proofread your poem for spelling, grammar, and capitalization errors.
- Make enough final copies of the villanelle for every team member and store yours in your writing portfolio.

Author's Purpose

If We Must Die
by Claude McKay

Old Ironsides
by Oliver Wendell Holmes

The Flying Cat
by Naomi Shihab Nye

The Solitary
by Sara Teasdale

Woman with Flower
by Naomi Long Madgett

A Work of Artifice
by Marge Piercy

Cinderella
by Anne Sexton

Ulysses
by Alfred, Lord Tennyson

Break, Break, Break
by Alfred, Lord Tennyson

Caged Bird
by Maya Angelou

INTRODUCTION

ABOUT THE LESSONS

Some authors and poets say that they write because they "have to." A force within them urges them to put words on paper for a variety of reasons. In some cases, the author has a clear public purpose—for example, to influence readers' opinions about a compelling issue. In other cases, an author's purpose is much more personal—for example, to clarify ideas or to share intense feelings.

The poems in this unit are divided into three groups. The poems in Group 1 all have clear purposes and themes. The poems in Group 2 have speakers with unmistakable attitudes that support the author's purpose. The poems in Group 3 can be analyzed and discussed from a number of different perspectives.

WRITING: DISCUSSING A POEM

At the end of this unit you will write a short essay in which you discuss a particular poem. In addition to discussing the various elements of the poem, you will give your opinion about how effectively the poet has used certain techniques to accomplish his or her purpose. Follow these steps to get started:

- Slowly page through this book. When you come upon a poem that you remember enjoying, write its title on a list. Take time to reread as many poems as possible in your review of the book. List no more than two or three poems from each unit.
- Analyze the reason or reasons why you chose each poem on your list. For example, perhaps you chose one poem because it expresses feelings that you have had yourself at times. Perhaps you chose another one because you particularly enjoy its imagery. Next to each poem on your list, record at least one reason why you chose it.
- Save your notes. You will use them later in the unit.

ABOUT THIS POET

Maya Angelou (1928–) is a woman of many talents. She is a poet, an author, a playwright, a play and movie producer, a director, an actor, and a singer. Born in St. Louis, Missouri, she was educated in public schools and studied dance and drama privately.

Angelou has taught modern dance in Israel and Italy and appeared in plays such as *Porgy and Bess*, *Cabaret for Freedom*, and *Look Away*, both on and off Broadway. She directed the film *All Day Long* and her own one-act musical, *And Still I Rise*. She also narrated and hosted an African American television series and lectured and taught at various universities. She has written autobiographies, poetry, plays, screenplays, television plays, and musical scores.

Angelou has described her remarkable life in five autobiographies. She told about her life up to age 16 in her first autobiography, *I Know Why the Caged Bird Sings*. Published in 1970, the book became a popular and critical success. Angelou has written four more autobiographies, taking readers through her late adolescence, her role in the civil rights era, and most recently her lengthy stay in Ghana, where she reflected on the importance of her African heritage as well as her identity as an American.

Angelou was nominated for the National Book Award in 1970 for *I Know Why the Caged Bird Sings* and for a Pulitzer Prize in 1972 for *Just Give Me a Cool Drink of Water 'Fore I Diiie*. She was nominated for a Tony Award in 1973 for her performance in *Look Away* and again in 1977 for her role in *Roots*. In addition, she won a Grammy Award for Best Spoken Word or Non-Traditional Album in 1994. On that album she recorded "On the Pulse of Morning," the original poem she read at the inauguration of President Bill Clinton in 1993.

AS YOU READ

As you read each poem in this unit, ask yourself these questions:

- Why has the poet written this poem? What message is he or she trying to communicate to readers?
- How well has the poet accomplished his or her purpose for writing? What techniques are particularly effective?
- How does the speaker's attitude affect the poem?
- How well does the tone of the poem support the theme and the author's purpose?

If We Must Die

by Claude McKay

ABOUT THE SELECTION

Claude McKay (1890–1948) was born in Jamaica and moved to the United States in 1912 to study agriculture at Alabama's Tuskegee Institute. He soon decided that he preferred writing to farming, however, and moved to New York City. In addition to writing poems, he published novels and short stories, often about the difficulties faced by people of African descent in the United States, Europe, and the Caribbean. McKay wrote this particular poem in response to a Harlem race riot in 1919. During World War II it became quite popular with members of both the American and British armed forces.

If we must die, let it not be like hogs
Hunted and penned in an inglorious spot,
While round us bark the mad and hungry dogs,
Making their mock at our accursèd lot.
If we must die, O let us nobly die,
So that our precious blood may not be shed
In vain; then even the monsters we defy
Shall be constrained to honor us though dead!
O kinsmen! we must meet the common foe!
Though far outnumbered let us show us brave,
And for their thousand blows deal one deathblow!
What though before us lies the open grave?
Like men we'll face the murderous, cowardly pack,
Pressed to the wall, dying, but fighting back!

Old Ironsides

by Oliver Wendell Holmes

ABOUT THE SELECTION

Oliver Wendell Holmes (1809–1884), born in Cambridge, Massachusetts, was a physician as well as a poet and an essayist. He received his M.D. degree from Harvard and later taught and served as dean of its medical school. His engaging and entertaining style of speaking made his classes quite popular at Harvard. Holmes eventually made use of his considerable speaking skills in public lectures on literature. In 1830, while still a student, he wrote "Old Ironsides" in support of an effort to save the frigate *Constitution,* a warship that had played a major role in the War of 1812. For more information about Holmes, see About This Poet at the beginning of Unit 2. This stirring poem aroused public support, and the ship was restored and put back into service instead of being destroyed as planned.

Ay, tear her tattered ensign[1] down!
Long has it waved on high,
And many an eye has danced to see
That banner in the sky;
Beneath it rung the battle shout,
And burst the cannon's roar;—
The meteor of the ocean air
Shall sweep the clouds no more!

---

[1] flag flown by a ship to show its nationality

Her deck, once red with heroes' blood,
Where knelt the vanquished[2] foe,
When winds were hurrying o'er the flood,
And waves were white below,
No more shall feel the victor's tread,
Or know the conquered knee;—
The harpies[3] of the shore shall pluck
The eagle of the sea!

O, better that her shattered hulk
Should sink beneath the wave;
Her thunders shook the mighty deep,
And there should be her grave;
Nail to the mast her holy flag,
Set every threadbare sail,
And give her to the god of storms,
The lightning and the gale!

[2] conquered; beaten

[3] mythological creatures, half-woman and half-bird, that steal from their victims

The Flying Cat

by Naomi Shihab Nye

ABOUT THE SELECTION

Naomi Shihab Nye (1952–) was born in St. Louis, Missouri. Her father is Palestinian, so while growing up Nye spent some time in the Middle East as well as in San Antonio, Texas. She has been a teacher, a songwriter, a poet, and a world traveler. Nye herself may be a world traveler, but according to the speaker in the following poem, the flying cat is not.

Never, in all your career of worrying, did you imagine
what worries could occur concerning the flying cat.
You are traveling to a distant city.
The cat must travel in a small box with holes.

Will the baggage compartment be pressurized?
Will a soldier's footlocker fall on the cat during take-off?
Will the cat freeze?

You ask these questions one by one, in different voices
over the phone. Sometimes you get an answer,
sometimes a click.
Now it's affecting everything you do.
At dinner you feel nauseous, like you're swallowing
at twenty thousand feet.
In dreams you wave fish-heads, but the cat has grown propellers,
the cat is spinning out of sight!

Will he faint when the plane lands?
Is the baggage compartment soundproofed?
Will the cat go deaf?

"Ma'am, if the cabin weren't pressurized, your cat would
explode."
And spoken in a droll[1] impersonal tone, as if
the explosion of cats were another statistic!

Hugging the cat before departure, you realize again
the private language of pain. He purrs. He trusts you.
He knows little of planets or satellites,
black holes in space or the weightless rise of fear.

[1] laughable; odd and amusing

The Solitary

by Sara Teasdale

ABOUT THE SELECTION

Sara Teasdale (1884–1933) was born in St. Louis, Missouri. After traveling to Europe and the Middle East she settled in New York City, where she lived in seclusion for many years. In 1918 she won the first Pulitzer Prize ever awarded for poetry for her volume *Love Songs.* Most of her poems revolve around themes of love, beauty, and death. As she grew older Teasdale withdrew more from society, just as the speaker in this poem seems to have done.

My heart has grown rich with the passing of years,
   I have less need now than when I was young
To share myself with every comer
   Or shape my thoughts into words with my tongue.

It is one to me that they come or go
   If I have myself and the drive of my will,
And strength to climb on a summer night
   And watch the stars swarm over the hill.

Let them think I love them more than I do,
   Let them think I care, though I go alone;
If it lifts their pride, what is it to me
   Who am self-complete as a flower or a stone.

Woman with Flower

by Naomi Long Madgett

ABOUT THE SELECTION

On the surface it seems that Naomi Long Madgett has written a poem about the proper treatment of a plant. But does the poem give advice that is more significant than simple gardening hints? Judge for yourself as you read this poem.

I wouldn't coax the plant if I were you,
Such watchful nurturing may do it
harm.
Let the soil rest from so much digging
And wait until it's dry before you water
it.
The leaf's inclined to find its own
direction;
Give it a chance to seek the sunlight for
itself.

Much growth is stunted by too careful
prodding,
Too eager tenderness.
The things we love we have to learn to
leave alone.

A Work of Artifice

by Marge Piercy

ABOUT THE SELECTION

Marge Piercy (1936–) was born in Detroit, Michigan. Since receiving her master's degree from Northwestern University, she has become a professional writer who gives readings, lectures, and workshops in colleges and universities across the United States. Her poetry has been recognized with awards including two Borestone Mountain Poetry Awards and the Literature Award from the Governor's Commission on the Status of Women in Massachusetts. Like "Woman with Flower," this poem seems to focus on caring for a plant—in this case a *bonsai.* You will soon recognize the poem's deeper meaning, however.

The bonsai tree
in the attractive pot
could have grown eighty feet tall
on the side of a mountain
till split by lightning.
But a gardener
carefully pruned it.
It is nine inches high.
Every day as he
whittles back the branches
the gardener croons,
It is your nature
to be small and cozy,
domestic and weak;
how lucky, little tree,
to have a pot to grow in.

With living creatures
one must begin very early
to dwarf their growth:
the bound feet,
the crippled brain,
the hair in curlers,
the hands you
love to touch.

Cinderella

by Anne Sexton

ABOUT THE SELECTION

Anne Sexton (1928–1974) was born in Newton, Massachusetts. At the suggestion of her psychiatrist she began writing poetry at the age of 28. Her poems are often intensely personal and intimate, so she is often considered to be part of a group of "confessional" poets. In 1966 Sexton won the Pulitzer Prize for poetry for her book *Live and Die.* In the following poem she retells a familiar fairy tale—but with attitude.

You always read about it:
the plumber with twelve children
who wins the Irish Sweepstakes.
From toilets to riches.
That story.

Or the nursemaid,
some luscious sweet from Denmark
who captures the oldest son's heart.
From diapers to Dior.[1]
That story.

Or a milkman who serves the wealthy,
eggs, cream, butter, yogurt, milk,
the white truck like an ambulance
who goes into real estate
and makes a pile.
From homogenized to martinis at lunch.

---

[1] a well-known fashion designer; the name of his line of clothing

Or the charwoman
who is on the bus when it cracks up
and collects enough from the insurance.
From mops to Bonwit Teller[2]
That story.

Once
the wife of a rich man was on her deathbed
and she said to her daughter Cinderella:
Be devout. Be good. Then I will smile
down from heaven in the seam of a cloud.
The man took another wife who had
two daughters, pretty enough
but with hearts like blackjacks.
Cinderella was their maid
She slept on the sooty hearth each night
and walked around looking like Al Jolson.[3]
Her father brought presents home from town,
jewels and gowns for the other women
but the twig of a tree for Cinderella.
She planted that twig on her mother's grave
and it grew to a tree where a white dove sat.
Whenever she wished for anything the dove
would drop it like an egg upon the ground.
The bird is important, my dears, so heed[4] him.

Next came the ball, as you all know.
It was a marriage market.
The prince was looking for a wife.
All but Cinderella were preparing
and gussying up for the big event.
Cinderella begged to go too.

---

[2] an expensive department store

[3] an entertainer of the early twentieth century who wore blackface makeup

[4] pay attention to

Her stepmother threw a dish of lentils
into the cinders and said: Pick them
up in an hour and you shall go.
The white dove brought all his friends;
all the warm wings of the fatherland came,
and picked up the lentils in a jiffy.
No, Cinderella, said the stepmother,
you have no clothes and cannot dance.
That's the way with stepmothers.

Cinderella went to the tree at the grave
and cried forth like a gospel singer:
Mama! Mama! My turtledove,
send me to the prince's ball!
The bird dropped down a golden dress
and delicate little gold slippers.
Rather a large package for a simple bird.
So she went. Which is no surprise.
Her stepmother and sisters didn't
recognize her without her cinder face
and the prince took her hand on the spot
and danced with no other the whole day.

As nightfall came she thought she'd better
get home. The prince walked her home
and she disappeared into the pigeon house
and although the prince took an axe and broke
it open she was gone. Back to her cinders.
These events repeated themselves for three days.
However on the third day the prince
covered the palace steps with cobbler's wax
and Cinderella's gold shoe stuck upon it.

Now he would find whom the shoe fit
and find his strange dancing girl for keeps.
He went to their house and the two sisters
were delighted because they had lovely feet.

The eldest went into a room to try the slipper on
but her big toe got in the way so she simply
sliced it off and put on the slipper.

The prince rode away with her until the white dove
told him to look at the blood pouring forth.
That is the way with amputations.
They don't just heal up like a wish.
The other sister cut off her heel
but the blood told as blood will.
The prince was getting tired.
He began to feel like a shoe salesman.
But he gave it one last try.
This time Cinderella fit into the shoe
like a love letter into its envelope.

At the wedding ceremony
the two sisters came to curry favor[5]
and the white dove pecked their eyes out.
Two hollow spots were left
like soup spoons.

Cinderella and the prince
lived, they say, happily ever after,
like two dolls in a museum case
never bothered by diapers or dust,
never arguing over the timing of an egg,
never telling the same story twice,
never getting a middle-aged spread,
their darling smiles pasted on for eternity,
Regular Bobbsey Twins.[6]
That story.

---

[5] act in such as way as to receive favors

[6] the always-happy main characters from a well-known series of children's books

Ulysses

by Alfred, Lord Tennyson

ABOUT THE SELECTION

Alfred, Lord Tennyson (1809–1892) served as England's esteemed poet laureate from 1850 until his death. He is known for his lyric poems, dramatic monologues, and long narratives. The speaker in this poem is Ulysses, king of Ithaca, who fought bravely during the Trojan War. After the war, he wandered for 10 years, facing disaster many times and surviving through a combination of wit and courage before returning home. Here he is speaking as an old man, a king reigning over a peaceful kingdom with his wife and his son Telemachus.

It little profits[1] that an idle king,
By this still hearth, among these barren crags,
Matched with an agèd wife, I mete[2] and dole[3]
Unequal laws unto a savage race
That hoard, and sleep, and feed, and know not me.
I cannot rest from travel; I will drink
Life to the lees.[4] All times I have enjoyed
Greatly, have suffered greatly, both with those
That loved me, and alone; on shore, and when
Through scudding drifts the rainy Hyades[5]

---

[1] benefits

[2] measure

[3] distribute or hand out

[4] end

[5] clustered stars in the Taurus constellation; the ancient Greeks expected rain when the Hyades rose with the sun

Vexed the dim sea. I am become a name;
For always roaming with a hungry heart
Much have I seen and known—cities of men
And manners, climates, councils, governments,
Myself not least, but honored of them all—
And drunk delight of battle with my peers,
Far on the ringing plains of windy Troy.
I am a part of all that I have met;
Yet all experience is an arch wherethrough
Gleams that untraveled world whose margin fades
Forever and forever when I move.
How dull it is to pause, to make an end,
To rust unburnished, not to shine in use!
As though to breathe were life! Life piled on life
Were all too little, and of one to me
Little remains; but every hour is saved
From that eternal silence, something more,
A bringer of new things; and vile it were
For some three suns to store and hoard myself,
And this gray spirit yearning in desire
To follow knowledge like a sinking star,
Beyond the utmost bound of human thought.
  This is my son, mine own Telemachus,
To whom I leave the scepter and the isle—
Well-loved of me, discerning to fulfill
This labor, by slow prudence to make mild
A rugged people, and through soft degrees
Subdue them to the useful and the good.
Most blameless is he, centered in the sphere
Of common duties, decent not to fail
In offices of tenderness, and pay
Meet adoration to my household gods,
When I am gone. He works his work, I mine.
  There lies the port; the vessel puffs her sail;
There gloom the dark, broad seas. My mariners,
Souls that have toiled, and wrought, and thought with me—
That ever with a frolic welcome took

The thunder and the sunshine, and opposed
Free hearts, free foreheads—you and I are old;
Old age hath yet his honor and his toil.
Death closes all; but something ere the end,
Some work of noble note, may yet be done,
Not unbecoming men that strove with Gods.
The lights begin to twinkle from the rocks;
The long day wanes, the low moon climbs; the deep[6]
Moans round with many voices. Come, my friends,
'Tis not too late to seek a newer world.
Push off, and sitting well in order smite
The sounding furrows;[7] for my purpose holds
To sail beyond the sunset, and the baths
Of all the western stars, until I die.
It may be that the gulfs will wash us down;
It may be we shall touch the Happy Isles,
And see the great Achilles, whom we knew.
Though much is taken, much abides; and though
We are not now that strength which in old days
Moved earth and heaven, that which we are, we are—
One equal temper of heroic hearts,
Made weak by time and fate, but strong in will
To strive, to seek, to find, and not to yield.

[6] the sea

[7] set off on the waves of the seas

Break, Break, Break

by Alfred, Lord Tennyson

ABOUT THE SELECTION

When Alfred, Lord Tennyson wrote this poem he was probably thinking about the death of his close friend Arthur Henry Hallam in 1833. After Hallam's death Tennyson was so depressed that he vowed not to publish any poetry for 10 years. After this period of silence he published a two-volume book called *Poems,* which was an immediate success. Another of Tennyson's major poems, *In Memoriam,* is also dedicated to the memory of Hallam. For more information about Tennyson, see the biographical note that precedes "Ulysses" in Group 2 of this unit.

Break, break, break,
  On thy cold gray stones, O Sea!
And I would that my tongue could utter
  The thoughts that arise in me.

O, well for the fisherman's boy,
  That he shouts with his sister at play!
O, well for the sailor lad,
  That he sings in his boat on the bay!

And the stately ships go on
  To their haven under the hill;
But O for the touch of a vanished hand,
  And the sound of a voice that is still!

Break, break, break,
  At the foot of thy crags, O Sea!
But the tender grace of a day that is dead
  Will never come back to me.

Caged Bird

by Maya Angelou

ABOUT THE SELECTION

Maya Angelou (1928–) has been a cook, a streetcar conductor, a waitress, a singer, an actress, a playwright, an editor, and a poet; and she has excelled at everything she has tried. In her simple and lyrical poetry, she often focuses on the problems faced by African Americans. You can learn more about Maya Angelou in About This Poet at the beginning of this unit. What theme, or message, do you think Angelou is trying to convey in this poem?

A free bird leaps
on the back of the wind
and floats downstream
till the current ends
and dips his wing
in the orange sun rays
and dares to claim the sky.

But a bird that stalks
down his narrow cage
can seldom see through
his bars of rage
his wings are clipped and
his feet are tied
so he opens his throat to sing.

The caged bird sings
with a fearful trill
of things unknown
but longed for still
and his tune is heard
on the distant hill
for the caged bird
sings of freedom.

The free bird thinks of another breeze
and the trade winds soft through the sighing trees
and the fat worms waiting on a dawn-bright lawn
and he names the sky his own.

UNDERSTANDING THE POEMS

Record your answers to these questions in your personal literature notebook. Follow the directions for each group.

GROUP 1

Reread the poems in Group 1 to complete these sentences.

Reviewing the Selection

1. The speaker in "Old Ironsides" recommends that instead of being destroyed slowly, the ship should be
   a. allowed to fall apart and sink.
   b. repaired and used again as a battleship.
   c. dismantled and the parts reused.
   d. blown up by cannon fire.

2. The speaker in "If We Must Die" urges readers to
   a. honor their enemies.
   b. mock their enemies.
   c. remember those who died before them.
   d. fight back nobly.

Interpreting the Selection

3. In "The Flying Cat" the speaker asks questions over the phone in different voices in order to
   a. catch the person who answers questions in a lie or a mistake.
   b. play a joke on the employee who answers the phone.
   c. cover up the fact that he or she has called so many times.
   d. see if different people would receive different answers.

Recognizing How Words Are Used

4. The rhyme scheme of the first stanza of "The Solitary" is
   a. *abab.*
   b. *abcb.*
   c. *abac.*
   d. *aabb.*

Appreciating Poetry

5. The main speaker in "The Flying Cat" is probably a
   a. woman who loves her cat.
   b. man who answers the phone for the airlines.
   c. little girl who is traveling somewhere with her parents.
   d. cat who is about to travel on a plane.

GROUP 2 Reread the poems in Group 2 to complete these sentences.

Reviewing the Selection

6. The bonsai tree in "A Work of Artifice" can never grow tall because a gardener
   a. refuses to give it enough light and water.
   b. tells it that it is meant to be small and cozy.
   c. prunes its branches every day.
   d. sings to it.

7. To convince the prince that she is the woman he danced with at the ball, the eldest sister in "Cinderella"
   a. slices off her heel so that the gold shoe fits her.
   b. slices off her big toe so that the gold shoe fits her.
   c. dances with him the same way that Cinderella had danced.
   d. gives the prince a love letter.

Interpreting the Selection

8. The speaker in "Ulysses" is encouraging his crew to
   a. sail with him to find new adventures.
   b. cooperate with his son in governing the kingdom.
   c. be content with remembering past adventures.
   d. ridicule people who never undertake dangerous adventures.

Recognizing How Words Are Used

9. An example of internal rhyme in "Woman with Flower" is
   a. "And wait until it's dry before you water/it."
   b. "I wouldn't coax the plant if I were you."
   c. "Give it a chance to seek the sunlight for/itself."
   d. "The leaf's inclined to find its own/direction."

Appreciating Poetry

10. The bonsai tree in "A Work of Artifice" is compared to a
   a. bolt of lightning because it is bent and crooked.
   b. woman because it is prevented from achieving its potential.
   c. small animal that needs to be protected.
   d. clay pot because it is little and fragile.

GROUP 3

Reread the poems in Group 3 to complete these sentences.

Reviewing the Selection

11. The speaker in "Break, Break, Break" is addressing
a. his friend who has died.
b. the sea.
c. a boy playing near the sea.
d. happier days that are now in the past.

12. The speaker in "Caged Bird" says that the free bird does all of the following *except*
a. leap on the wind's back.
b. sing with a fearful trill.
c. think of the trade winds.
d. name the sky his own.

Interpreting the Selection

13. The speaker in "Break, Break, Break" mentions the happy activities of the fisherman's boy and the sailor lad to
a. suggest that everyone reacts differently to death.
b. identify the relatives of the person who died.
c. show how callous and cruel people can be.
d. contrast their joy and his or her own unhappiness.

Recognizing How Words Are Used

14. The lines "A free bird leaps/on the back of the wind/and floats downstream/till the current ends" from "Caged Bird" contain an example of
a. near rhyme.
b. onomatopoeia.
c. alliteration.
d. repetition.

Appreciating Poetry

15. The speaker in "Break, Break, Break" is feeling
a. carefree.
b. angry.
c. sorrowful.
d. proud.

Now check your answers with your teacher. Study the questions you answered incorrectly. What types of questions were they? Talk with your teacher about ways to work on those skills.

Author's Purpose

When teenagers ask to borrow the family car, they know that the words they choose and the attitudes they display will affect the outcome of their request. When employees ask for raises, they prepare reasons for why their hard work deserves to be rewarded. When candidates campaign for votes, they say what they think their voters want to hear. Before any of these people speak, they understand their purposes clearly, and they organize their thoughts and words in order to achieve those purposes.

Poets, too, have definite purposes in mind when they write their poems. Often they wish to share with their audiences messages or insights about life. These messages or insights are called *themes*. All the elements in a poem work together to support the central theme. One element that is important in conveying the theme is the *tone*, or attitude, of the speaker in the poem.

In the following lessons you will examine the author's purpose in a variety of poems. You also will look at each poem's theme and tone and will focus on these ideas:

1. The author's purpose is the reason why he or she wrote the poem. In many poems careful examination of the theme enables readers to understand the author's purpose.

2. The tone of the speaker—his or her attitude toward the subject or the audience—should support the theme and the author's purpose.

3. A fair evaluation of a poem should be based not only on personal opinion but also on how well the poem meets its goals and objective criteria.

LESSON 1 AUTHOR'S PURPOSE AND THEME

Have you ever found yourself wondering why poets—who have messages to share and reasons for writing—don't just come out and say what they mean in a more straightforward manner? For example, take Oliver Wendell Holmes. He wrote the poem "Old

Ironsides" as part of an effort to save the dilapidated war frigate *Constitution*. If he had wanted the old ship to be preserved, why didn't he simply write, "I think the *Constitution* should be saved no matter what it costs"? Even though he was young, his opinion might have persuaded a few people to join the fight to preserve the ship. If he had supplied a few logical reasons to support his opinion, he might have won over a few more supporters. But Holmes understood that the intensity of a poem can convey a theme in a more powerful and personal way. Instead of appealing to people's heads by writing his ideas in prose, Holmes wrote a poem that would appeal to people's hearts. In his poem he reminds Americans that *Old Ironsides* was the scene of past valor. He tries to persuade them that the ship is deserving of a better fate than being scrapped. He begins by seemingly advocating an action that is the opposite of what he really wants:

> Ay, tear her tattered ensign down!
> Long has it waved on high,
> And many an eye has danced to see
> That banner in the sky;
> Beneath it rung the battle shout,
> And burst the cannon's roar;—
> The meteor of the ocean air
> Shall sweep the clouds no more!

Later in the poem Holmes claims that it would be better to let the ship sink than to allow thieves to carry off its parts, bit by bit. His theme is that the ship is so precious and noble that it should not be despoiled by being treated like any ordinary ship. That theme supports his purpose: the preservation of the ship. By writing a poem instead of simply stating his opinion in everyday language, he won over the hearts of enough Americans to accomplish his purpose.

Not all poems are written to influence popular opinion. Some poets simply want to share an idea that they think is somehow significant. Look, for example, at "The Flying Cat" by Naomi Shihab Nye. Although she doesn't seem particularly pleased with the attitude of the airline employee who drolly says, "Ma'am, if the cabin weren't pressurized, your cat would explode," her purpose is not to change the attitudes of airline employees or to instigate a demand for changes in the treatment of animals. Instead she wants readers to focus on what she has learned about herself and her pet:

> Hugging the cat before departure, you realize again
> the private language of pain. He purrs. He trusts you.
> He knows little of planets or satellites,
> black holes in space or the weightless rise of fear.

The author's purpose may be to share her insight about how much people love their pets and worry about them sometimes. The simple theme of the speaker's concern about her pet supports an equally simple and personal purpose.

EXERCISE 1

Reread "If We Must Die" and "The Solitary." Then use what you have learned in this lesson to answer these questions:

1. In your own words state the theme of "If We Must Die." Why do you think the poet wrote this poem?
2. Would you describe the purpose of "The Solitary" as a plea to change your behavior or a private and personal statement? To answer that question, decide whether the speaker wants to persuade readers to act in a certain way or if he or she is simply sharing a personal point of view.
3. What insight about life has the speaker in "The Solitary" learned "with the passing of years"?

Now check your answers with your teacher. Review this part of the lesson if you don't understand why an answer was incorrect.

WRITING ON YOUR OWN 

In the previous writing exercise you reviewed all the poems in this book and listed the ones you like best. Now you will focus on the themes of those poems. Follow these steps:

- Review your list of chosen poems and circle the ones with strong themes. Next to each circled poem, briefly summarize its theme.
- Now choose the one poem that you would like to focus on in your essay. Read the poem again and decide on at least three elements that you feel the poet handled well. Write some notes about these elements that you can use to write your essay.

TONE

Internet users are regularly warned that the tone of written words can be misunderstood. E-mail veterans remind new users that WRITING IN ALL CAPITAL LETTERS makes readers feel as if they are being SHOUTED AT.

New users also quickly learn that sarcasm doesn't always translate well and can be easily mistaken for anger or bitterness. That is why symbols suggesting smiling :-) or sarcastic ;-) faces are often added to take the bite out of jokes that might otherwise come across as mean. Users are reminded that any criticism or show of temper is magnified in an e-mail message. Writing with these rules in mind, e-mailers can be fairly confident that they are communicating the messages they actually intend.

Now consider the formidable task that poets face. Their poems can be misunderstood just as easily as Internet messages are. And poets, like e-mailers, have no choice: When they want to share an idea, a belief, or an experience, they can't use their voices to communicate. They must rely on the power of the written word to convey their emotions and attitudes. To help convey their messages, poets use a speaker or speakers. The attitudes of the speakers are crucial in conveying the poets' themes and accomplishing their purposes for writing. For example, in "A Work of Artifice" Marge Piercy has chosen a speaker who seems angry and bitter. In these lines the speaker uses *irony*, the technique of saying the opposite of what is meant:

> With living creatures
> one must begin very early
> to dwarf their growth:
> the bound feet,
> the crippled brain,
> the hair in curlers,
> the hands you
> love to touch.

In reality the speaker is outraged that women have been deprived of the right to grow and develop naturally, but instead of shouting his or her anger the speaker seethes. The speaker's tone is sarcastic and cutting, and it supports the author's purpose of holding up to ridicule the senseless misuse and denial of women's potential.

While the speaker in "A Work of Artifice" is angry, the speaker in Anne Sexton's "Cinderella" is cynical. He or she looks at the world and finds patterns that seem both pointless and unchangeable:

> You always read about it:
> the plumber with twelve children
> who wins the Irish Sweepstakes.
> From toilets to riches.
> That story.
>
> Or the nursemaid,
> some luscious sweet from Denmark
> who captures the oldest son's heart.
> From diapers to Dior.
> That story.

The speaker is world-weary and jaded. He or she has seen and heard it all. Although the speaker is telling a familiar fairy tale, his or her tone turns the story from innocent and romantic to tacky and ridiculous. Who can believe the ending of this tale, as the speaker tells it?

> Cinderella and the prince
> lived, they say, happily ever after,
> like two dolls in a museum case
> never bothered by diapers or dust,
> never arguing over the timing of an egg,
> never telling the same story twice,
> never getting a middle-aged spread,
> their darling smiles pasted on for eternity,
> Regular Bobbsey Twins.
> That story.

The tone of the speaker in Tennyson's "Ulysses" differs sharply from those of the speakers in the previous two poems. In this poem you meet a speaker who is unashamedly hopeful and idealistic. You are swept away by his or her optimism tempered by realism. After reading these closing lines you, too, feel like a king who can do great things:

> Death closes all; but something ere the end,
> Some work of noble note, may yet be done,
> Not unbecoming men that strove with Gods.
> The lights begin to twinkle from the rocks;
> The long day wanes, the low moon climbs; the deep
> Moans round with many voices. Come, my friends,
> 'Tis not too late to seek a newer world. . . .
> Though much is taken, much abides; and though
> We are not now that strength which in old days
> Moved earth and heaven, that which we are, we are—
> One equal temper of heroic hearts,
> Made weak by time and fate, but strong in will
> To strive, to seek, to find, and not to yield.

EXERCISE 2

Reread "Woman with Flower" by Naomi Long Madgett. Then use what you have learned in this lesson to answer these questions:

1. Both this poem and "A Work of Artifice" lead us to see similarities between the way we treat plants and the way we treat humans. What advice does the speaker in "Woman with Flower" give to those who would grow healthy plants and healthy human beings?
2. How is the speaker's tone in this poem different from that of the speaker in "A Work of Artifice"? What is the theme of the poem, and how does the tone of the speaker support the theme?

Now check your answers with your teacher. Review this part of the lesson if you don't understand why an answer was incorrect.

WRITING ON YOUR OWN 

In Anne Sexton's poem "Cinderella" the speaker retells the familiar fairy tale in a cynical tone and from a thoroughly modern point of view. In this exercise you will decide on the tone of the speaker in your chosen poem. Follow these steps:

- Reread the poem you chose to focus on in Writing on Your Own 1.
- Decide who the speaker of the poem might be and what tone he or she conveys. Jot down a few words or phrases to describe the speaker's tone, attitude, and point of view.
- Write a few sentences that tell whether or not you think the speaker's tone is appropriate and effective in this particular poem. Then save your notes for the next writing exercise.

LESSON 3 DISCUSSING A POEM

Once you have eaten gourmet food, fast-food restaurants don't quite measure up anymore. Once you have heard a symphony, harmonica music just doesn't give you the thrill it did before. And now that you have read many good poems, you will find that overly sentimental or cliché-ridden poems do not please you the way they once did. In this book you have begun to learn what makes poems good. Now, using that knowledge, you should be able to evaluate poetry and select poems that satisfy particular criteria.

Evaluating a poem involves both thought and feeling, both your brain and your heart. Your brain allows you to analyze the poem, element by element. Perhaps it tells you that the poet excelled in his or her use of clever or entertaining rhyme and rhythm or that the figures of speech were eye-opening and effective. Sometimes you can use logic to decide whether the poet has accomplished his or her purpose for writing. While your mind can appreciate the skill of the poet in meeting your standards for a superior poem, it provides only half of the evaluation. The poem also must speak to your emotions. It must strike a chord in you or state a theme that resonates with your own life and experiences. For this reason a discussion of a poem should include both your objective, analytic reaction and your subjective, emotional reaction.

In the following short essay a writer discusses the poem "Break, Break, Break." The writer begins with a general statement about the poem. Then he or she launches into a summary of the poem for those who have never read it. Element by element, the writer analyzes the poet's treatment of several different elements. Finally, the writer concludes with a statement explaining his or her opinion of the poem. Read the essay to find out which elements of the poem the writer found particularly noteworthy.

> "Break, Break, Break" by Alfred, Lord Tennyson is a sad lament for a lost friend. Many people think that Tennyson wrote this poem to express his deep sense of loss over the

death of his friend Arthur Hallam. In the poem a speaker near a rocky shore addresses the sea as if it were a person. While expressing his or her grief the speaker notices others who are still happily going about their daily business, unaware of the speaker's heartbreak. The speaker seems to find some solace in the unchanging sea whose waves break over and over again on "cold gray stones." He or she sadly comes to realize, however, that the past is gone, never to return.

Tennyson has made effective use of sounds in this poem. "Break, Break, Break" follows a traditional form which uses a clear and regular rhythm and an easy-to-follow rhyme scheme. Most lines have three strong beats; the rhyme scheme follows a simple *abcb* pattern. This traditional approach coordinates well with the personality of the speaker, who seems to be focusing on the past rather than the future as he or she remembers the friend. At the beginning of the poem and again in the last stanza, the speaker says the word *break* three times. This repetition imitates the incessant sound of waves breaking on the shore.

Tennyson uses a special kind of metaphor called apostrophe when he has the speaker talk directly to the sea. This figure of speech helps convey the speaker's loneliness, which he or she hopes the sea can somehow heal. Another way Tennyson shows the speaker's feelings is by having the speaker notice the children at play, the singing sailor, and the ships continuing their daily routines, thereby emphasizing how different the speaker's feelings are from everyone else's.

Although this poem is sad I enjoyed it. It makes me feel less lonely to know that other people feel unhappy at times, and that if I try, I can find comfort in nature. I also like the drama in this poem and the speaker's willingness to show his or her emotions. Finally, the effective use of rhythm and rhyme in this poem will probably help me remember it for a long time to come.

The writer of this essay first discusses what he or she considers to be the strengths of the poem—its use of sounds, such as rhythm, rhyme, and repetition; its effective use of figurative language; its truthful theme; and a speaker with whose feelings the writer can identify. The writer than concludes the essay by sharing his or her personal, subjective reaction to the poem.

EXERCISE 3

Reread the poems in Group 3. Then use what you have learned in this lesson to answer these questions:

1. If you were to write an essay about "Caged Bird," on which elements of poetry would you concentrate? Choose at least two of the following elements and explain why focusing on them would be appropriate in a discussion of this poem: imagery; sensory details and concrete language; sounds, including rhythm and rhyme, alliteration, assonance, consonance, and onomatopoeia; figurative language; mood; theme; tone; speaker; author's purpose.
2. Which of the poems in this unit would you choose to share with a friend who enjoys poetry? Why do you think he or she would enjoy those particular poems?

Now check your answers with your teacher. Review this part of the lesson if you don't understand why an answer was incorrect.

WRITING ON YOUR OWN 3

In previous writing exercises you listed your favorite poems, circled the ones with strong themes, chose one poem to focus on in your essay, and described its speaker and tone. Now you will do some more planning for your essay. Follow these steps:

- Write the title of your chosen poem in a circle at the center of a sheet of paper. Create a concept map, or web, by drawing eight more circles around the title and connecting each outer circle to the central circle with a line. Then write these words or phrases in the eight circles: *speaker, sensory images and concrete language, sounds, figurative language, mood, form, theme, tone.*
- Now think about how each of these elements is treated in your chosen poem and record your ideas, as in the example below. When you are finished you will have developed concepts that you can use to write your final essay. For some categories, you will have little or nothing to say because the strengths of the poem lie in its treatment of other elements.

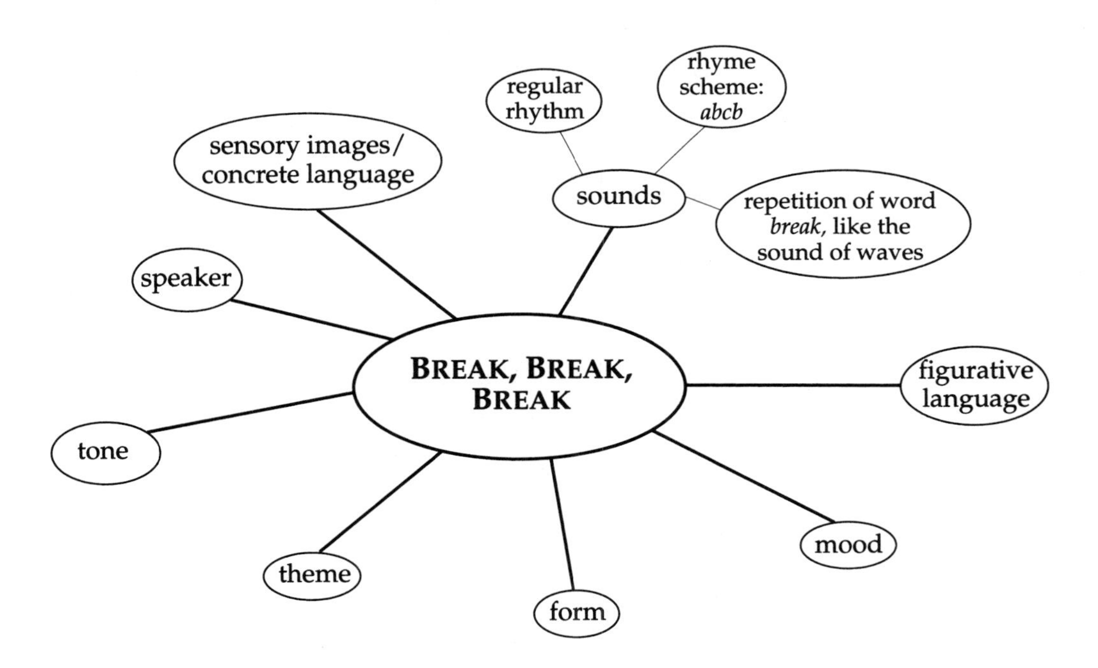

DISCUSSION GUIDES

1. Do you know why the *Constitution* was called "Old Ironsides"? What was the ship's role in the War of 1812? Why would people feel so strongly about preserving this particular ship? Do some research on the *Constitution* and the War of 1812 and summarize your findings in a short report to the rest of the class.

2. In "A Work of Artifice" the speaker is clearly angry about the treatment of women. Not only women are hemmed in and limited by social pressures, however. In a small group, discuss how society limits the growth of other groups as well. Consider what society expects from each group and how it treats those who don't meet those expectations.

3. Earlier in this unit you made a list of your favorite poems from this book. Now, with a small group of classmates, create a collection of the group's favorite poems. Share your list of poems with the group and listen as they share theirs. Have a recording secretary keep track of the poems that come up on more than one list. Then choose 10 poems that you all agree should be in the collection. To persuade others to include a poem, explain why you like it. When your group has decided on your 10 final choices, compile the poems and create your collection. Share your collection with other groups in the class. It will be interesting to see which poems, if any, appear in every collection.

4. At the end of Unit 1 your class developed a questionnaire about poetry. Now that your study of poetry is nearing an end, take a few moments to answer the survey questions again. After the results are tabulated, see if your class's attitudes toward and knowledge of poetry have changed.

WRITE AN ESSAY ABOUT A POEM

In this unit you have learned how theme and tone contribute to accomplishing the author's purpose. You also have learned how to analyze a poem so that you can discuss it objectively. Now you will write a short essay about a particular poem.

Follow these steps to write your essay. If you have questions about the writing process, refer to Using the Writing Process on page 245.

- Assemble and review the work you did for all the writing exercises in this unit: 1) a list of your favorite poems from this book and the reasons why you selected them, 2) a list of poems with strong themes and notes on three elements that were handled well in one poem, 3) a list of words or phrases that describe the speaker's tone and attitude; 4) a concept map that analyzes a poem with regard to eight major elements.
- In the previous writing exercise, you began analyzing a particular poem. Now you will write about that poem in your essay.
- Using your notes and the concept map that you developed, write the first draft of your essay. Begin with a general statement that suggests your opinion of the poem. Then summarize the poem briefly. Summarizing will help those who have not read the poem, and it will help you decide what is most essential about the poem .
- Next, element by element, explain the strengths of the poem, providing supporting evidence for each of your opinions. Discuss only the elements that are relevant to your particular poem. Conclude with a general statement about why you like or dislike the poem.
- Proofread your essay for spelling, grammar, punctuation, capitalization, and formatting errors. Then make a final copy to save in your writing portfolio. If any of your classmates have written about the same poem, you may want to read each other's essays to see how your evaluations are alike and different.

USING THE WRITING PROCESS

This reference section explains the major steps in the writing process. It will help you complete the writing exercises in this book. Read the information carefully so you can understand the process thoroughly. Whenever you need a quick review of important things to think about when you write, refer to the handy checklist on page 251.

Most tasks worth doing have several steps. For example, houses can be built only after the builder follows a number of complicated, logical steps. Moviemakers must go through a series of steps before releasing a film. Even a task as simple as making a peanut butter and jelly sandwich requires that the sandwich maker perform specific steps in order. So it should be no surprise that anyone who wants to write a good story, play, poem, report, or article must follow certain steps too. Taken together, the steps a writer follows are called the *writing process*.

STAGE 1: Prewriting

Prewriting consists of all the preparation you do before you put a single word down on paper. There are many decisions that you must make in order to make your writing as interesting, logical, and easy to read as possible. Here are the steps you should take before you begin to write:

1. **Decide on your audience.** Who will read your writing? Will your audience be your teacher? Will it be readers of the school newspaper? Or will your audience be family or friends? Your writing will change, depending on who you think your audience will be.

2. **Decide on your purpose.** Why are you writing? Do you want to teach your audience something? Do you want to entertain them? Do you want to change someone's mind about an issue? Think about your purpose before you begin to write.

3. **Think about possible topics.** What are some topics that interest you? Make a list of topics that you are familiar with and might

like to write about. Make another list of topics that interest you and that you want to learn about.

One technique that helps some writers at this stage is *brainstorming.* When you brainstorm, you let your mind wander freely. Without judging your ideas first, scribble them down as they come to you—even if they seem silly or farfetched. Good ideas often develop from unusual thoughts.

If you're having trouble coming up with ideas by yourself, brainstorm with a partner or a group of classmates. Jot down everyone's ideas as they say them. Brainstorm-ing alone or with others should give you a long list of possible writing topics.

4. **Choose and narrow your topic.** Once you have chosen a topic, you will probably find that it is impossible to cover every aspect of it in one piece of writing. Say, for example, you have chosen to write about the possibility of life on other planets. In a single piece of writing, you could not possibly include everything that has been researched about extraterrestrial life. Therefore you must choose one or two aspects to focus on, such as alleged sightings in the United States or worldwide organizations that study extraterrestrial life. Otherwise you might overload your writing with too many ideas. Concentrate on telling about a few things thoroughly and well.

5. **Research your topic.** You probably have had experience using an encyclopedia, the library, or the Internet to look up information for factual reports. But even when you write fictional stories, you often need to do some research. In a story set during the Civil War, for example, your characters wouldn't use pocket cameras or wear suits of armor. In order to make your story as accurate and believable as possible, you would have to research how Americans lived and dressed during the years of the Civil War.

   To conduct your research, you may want to use books, magazines, newspapers, reference works, or electronic sources, such as the Internet. Some topics may require you to interview knowledgeable people. For realistic stories set in the present time, you may find that the best research is simple observation of everyday life. Thorough research will help ensure that your facts and details are accurate.

6. **Organize your research.** Once you have the facts, ideas, and details, you need to decide how to arrange them. Which order will you choose? No matter what you are writing, it is always helpful to begin with a written plan. If you are writing a story, you probably will tell it in time order. Make a list of the major story events, arranged from first to last.

   Arranging details in time order is not the only way to organize information, however. Some writers start by making *lists* (informal outlines) of the facts and ideas they have gathered. Then they rearrange the items on their lists until they have the order that will work well in their writing.

   Other writers make formal *outlines,* designating the most important ideas with roman numerals (I, II, III, IV, and so on) and related details with letters and numerals (A, B, C; 1, 2, 3; a, b, c; and so on). An outline is a more formal version of a list, and like the items in a list, the items in an outline can be rearranged until you decide on a logical order. Both outlines and lists help you organize and group your ideas.

   Mapping or *clustering* is another helpful technique used by many writers. With this method, you write a main idea in the center of a cluster and then surround it with facts and ideas connected to that idea. Following is an example of a cluster map:

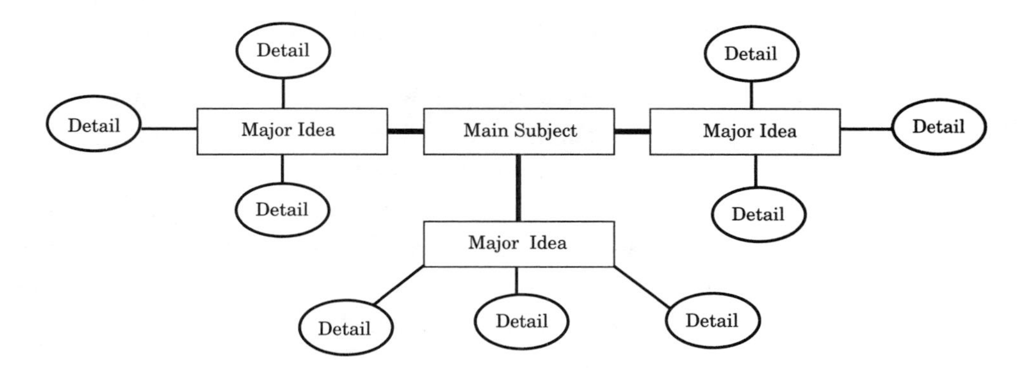

STAGE 2: Writing

1. **Get started.** Begin your writing with an introductory sentence or paragraph. A good introduction can become a guide for the rest of your piece. For ideas on good opening sentences, take a look at some of your favorite stories or magazine articles.

   Your introduction should give your audience a hint about what is coming next. If you are writing a story, your introduction should set the tone and mood. It should reveal the narrator's point of view; and it may introduce the main characters, the setting, and your purpose for writing. Do the best you can with your introduction, but remember that if you wish to, you can always change it later.

2. **Keep writing.** Get your thoughts down as quickly as possible, referring to your prewriting notes to keep you on track. Later, when you are done with this *rough draft,* you will have a chance to revise and polish your work to make it as clear and accurate as possible. For right now, however, don't stop for spelling, grammar, or exact wording problems. Come as close as you can to what you want to say, but don't let yourself get bogged down in details.

STAGE 3: Revising

Now you're ready to revise your work. Careful revision includes editing and reorganizing that can make a big difference in the final product. You may wish to get feedback from your classmates or your teacher about how to revise your work.

1. **Revise and edit your work.** When you are revising and editing, ask yourself these questions:
   - Did I follow my prewriting plan? Reread your entire first draft. Compare it to your original plan. Did you skip anything important? If you added an idea, did it work logically with the rest of your plan? Even if you decide that your prewriting plan is no longer what you want, it may include ideas you don't want to lose.

- Is my writing clear and logical? Does one idea follow the other in a sensible order? Do you want to change the order or add ideas to make the organization clearer?
- Is my language clear and interesting? Have you chosen exact verbs, nouns, and adjectives? For example, have you used forms of the verb *to be (is, are, being, become)* more often than you should? If so, replace them or change your sentence to make them unnecessary. Include precise action words such as *raced*, *hiked*, *zoomed*, and *hurried* in place of the overused verb *went.* Instead of using vague nouns such as *water* and *green,* choose exact ones such as *cascade* or *pond* and *lime.* Replace common adjectives such as *beautiful* and *nice* with precise ones such as *elegant, gorgeous,* and *lovely*.
- Is my writing clear and to the point? Take out words that repeat the same ideas. For example, don't use both *liberty* and *freedom.* These words are synonyms. Choose one word or the other.

2. **Proofread for errors in spelling, grammar, capitalization, and punctuation.** Anyone reading your writing will notice such errors immediately. These errors can confuse your readers or make them lose interest in what they are reading.

   If you are in doubt about the spelling of a word, look it up or ask someone for help. If you are unsure about your grammar, read your writing aloud and listen carefully. Does anything sound wrong? Check with a friend or classmate if you need a second opinion—or refer to a grammar handbook.

   Make sure every group of words is a complete sentence. Are any of your sentences run-ons? Do proper nouns begin with capital letters? Is the first word of every sentence capitalized? Do all your sentences have the correct end marks? Should you add any other punctuation to your writing to make your ideas even clearer? If your writing includes dialogue, have you used quotation marks correctly?

3. **Make a clean final draft to share.** After you are satisfied with your writing, it is time to share it with your audience. If you are lucky

enough to be composing on a computer, you can print out a final copy easily, after running a spell-check. If you are writing your final draft by hand, make sure your handwriting is clear and easy to read. Leave margins on either side of the page. You may want to skip every other line. Make your writing look inviting to your readers. After all, you put a lot of work into this piece. It's important that someone read and enjoy it.

A WRITING CHECKLIST

Ask yourself these questions before beginning a writing assignment:

- Have I chosen a topic that is both interesting and manageable? Should I narrow it so I can cover it in the space that I have?
- Do I have a clear prewriting plan?
- What should I do to gather my facts and ideas? read? interview? observe?
- How will I organize my ideas? In a list? an outline? a cluster map?
- Do I have an opening sentence or paragraph that will pull my readers in?
- Do I need to add more information? switch the order of paragraphs? take out unnecessary information?

Ask yourself these questions after completing a writing assignment:

- Did I use my prewriting plan?
- Is the organization of my writing clear? Should I move, add, or delete any paragraphs or sentences to make the ideas flow more logically?
- Do all the sentences in one paragraph relate to one idea?
- Have I used active, precise words? Is my language interesting? Do the words say what I mean to say?
- Are all the words spelled correctly?
- Have I used correct grammar, capitalization, punctuation, and formatting?
- Is my final draft legible, clean, and attractive?

GLOSSARY OF LITERARY TERMS

This glossary includes definitions for important literary terms that are introduced in this book. Boldfaced words within the definitions are other terms that appear in the glossary.

alliteration the repetition of the same sounds in words that are close together. These sounds are usually consonant sounds that occur at the beginnings of words, but they also can occur within words.

anapest a metrical **foot** in which two unstressed syllables are followed by a stressed syllable (∪ ∪ /).

apostrophe the technique of addressing a thing or an absent person.

assonance the repetition of vowel sounds within words.

audience the particular person or group that a writer is addressing.

author's purpose the reason why an author writes. Four common author's purposes are to entertain, to inform, to persuade, and to express feelings or opinions.

blank verse an unrhymed poem written in **iambic pentameter.**

character a person, animal, or object that carries out the action of a poem.

cliché an overused phrase or expression.

concrete language words and phrases that describe things that readers can experience with their senses. *See* **image** and **sensory detail.**

concrete poem a poem whose shape resembles the object it describes. This shape helps contribute to the meaning of the poem. *See* **iconograph.**

connotation the emotion that a word arouses or the meaning it suggests beyond its **denotation**, or dictionary meaning.

consonance a technique in which the consonant sounds at the ends of stressed syllables stay the same but the vowel sounds preceding them change, as in *pitter/patter* and *break/stick*.

couplet a pair of lines that rhyme.

dactyl a metrical **foot** in which a stressed syllable is followed by two unstressed syllables (/ ∪ ∪).

denotation the literal, dictionary meaning of a word.

dialect a version of a language spoken in one place or time, by one group of people.

dialogue a conversation between two characters.

dramatic monologue a poem with a single speaker who is engaged in a dramatic situation.

end rhyme rhyme that occurs at the ends of lines of poetry.

extended metaphor a special kind of metaphor that involves the entire poem. The individual metaphors within the poem contribute directly to the main metaphor. *See* **figure of speech, figurative language, metaphor,** and **implied metaphor.**

feminine rhyme rhyming words that consist of a stressed syllable followed by one or more unstressed syllables, as in *neighbor* and *labor*. Feminine rhymes also can be made from two or more words together, as in *limit* and *dim it*.

figurative language words and phrases used in such a way as to suggest something more than just their usual, dictionary meanings. *See* **figure of speech.**

figure of speech a word or phrase that suggests meanings other than the usual, dictionary meaning. Most figures of speech involve comparisons. Some figures of speech are **simile, metaphor, hyperbole,** and **personification**.

first-person point of view the vantage point, or perspective, in which the speaker is the person or character telling the story. When relating experiences from a first-person point of view, the speaker uses words such as *I*, *me*, and *we*. *See* **point of view** and **third-person point of view.**

foot the unit in which **meter** is measured. A foot consists of at least one stressed syllable and one or more unstressed syllables. The number of feet in a line of poetry equals the number of stressed syllables. *See* **scanning** and **stress.**

free verse poetry that does not have fixed **rhythm, rhyme, meter,** or line length. A poet using free verse is free to change patterns or to use no pattern at all.

hokku, or haiku a 3-line poem with 17 syllables. The first and third lines have 5 syllables each, and the second line has 7 syllables. The haiku, created first in Japan, expresses an experience by presenting one striking image.

hyperbole a **figure of speech** that exaggerates the truth to emphasize an idea or feeling. *See* **figurative language.**

iamb a metrical **foot** consisting of one stressed and one unstressed syllable in which the unstressed syllable regularly comes first (∪ /). *See* **meter** and **iambic pentameter.**

iambic pentameter a line of poetry that contains five iambic feet. In English poetry iambic pentameter is used more often than any other **meter.**

iconograph a poem that is written in the shape of the object it describes. *See* **concrete poem.**

image a mental picture created with words or phrases. Images can appeal to any of the senses—sight, hearing, taste, smell, and touch. Some images appeal to more than one sense.

imagery all the **images** that are created in a poem.

implied metaphor a kind of **metaphor,** also called *implicit metaphor,* in which one of the things being compared is not directly stated but is suggested by the context. "The shoppers swarmed into the store as soon as the doors opened" is an example of an implied metaphor in which the shoppers are indirectly compared to bees by the use of the word *swarmed.* *See* **figure of speech, figurative language,** and **extended metaphor.**

internal rhyme a rhyme that occurs when a word within a line rhymes with another word in the same line.

irony the contrast between what is said and what is really meant or between what happens and what was expected to happen.

limerick a short, humorous poem with five lines. Lines one, two, and five have three metric feet and lines three and four have two feet. The rhyme scheme is *aabba.*

lyric poem a poem that has a single speaker and expresses a deeply felt thought or emotion. Lyric poems have a musical quality. Often in a lyric poem, the speaker does not have a specific audience, but instead is addressing himself or herself.

masculine rhyme rhyming words with one syllable or one stressed syllable, as in *road* and *hoed* or *around* and *ground*.

metaphor a **figure of speech** in which one thing is spoken about as if it were another, unlike thing. A metaphor helps readers *see* the similarities between these two things. *See* **figurative language, extended metaphor,** and **implied metaphor.**

meter the regular rhythmic pattern of stressed and unstressed syllables in a line of poetry. Meter is counted in feet. The most common meter in English poetry is **iambic pentameter.** *See* **foot** and **stress.**

monologue a poem in which only one speaker talks. *See* **dramatic monologue.**

mood the general feeling or atmosphere created by a poem.

narrative poem a poem that tells a story.

narrator the **speaker** who tells the story in a narrative poem.

near-rhyme a sound technique in which words with matching consonant sounds (**consonance**) or matching vowel sounds (**assonance**) are substituted for true rhymes, as in these word pairs: **wind/end** and **boat/hope.**

onomatopoeia the use of words whose sounds imitate or suggest their meanings. Examples: **crash, buzz,** and **hiss.**

pentameter a five-foot line. *See* **foot** and **meter.**

persona the character who speaks in a poem. The poet speaks to the reader using that character's voice. *See* **speaker.**

personification a **figure of speech** in which an animal, an object, or an idea is given human qualities. *See* **figurative language.**

point of view vantage point from which a poem is written or a story is told. In a piece of literature written from a **first-person point of view,** the speaker uses words such as *I*, *me*, and *we*. In a piece written from the **third-person point of view,** the speaker uses the words *he*, *she*, and *they*.

prose the ordinary form of written or spoken language, without any rhyme or regular rhythm. Short stories, novels, and essays are written in prose.

quatrain a four-line **stanza** in a poem.

refrain one or more lines that are repeated in a poem or a song.

repetition the use of a sound, word, phrase, line, or stanza two or more times in a poem. *See* **refrain.**

rhyme the repetition of ending sounds in two or more words. *See* **end rhyme, near-rhyme, masculine rhyme,** and **feminine rhyme.**

rhyme scheme the pattern of **end rhyme** in a poem. The rhyme scheme can be determined if words at the ends of two or more lines rhyme. The rhyme scheme is shown by assigning a different letter of the alphabet to each line-end sound in a stanza. Lines that rhyme are given the same letter. For example, if the first and third lines rhyme and the second and fourth lines rhyme, the rhyme scheme is *abab*.

rhythm the pattern of stressed and unstressed syllables in a poem. *See* **stress.**

scanning counting the feet, or number and arrangement of stressed and unstressed syllables in a line, to determine the **meter.** *See* **foot** and **stress.**

sensory detail words or phrases that describe the way things look, sound, taste, smell, or feel. Many sensory details together can create a **sensory image.**

sensory image *See* **image.**

setting the time or place of the action in a poem or a story.

simile a **figure of speech** that compares two unlike things, using the word *like*, *as*, *appear*, or *seem*. *See* **figurative language.**

sonnet a fourteen-line poem with a fixed pattern of rhythm and meter that follows one of several **rhyme schemes.** A Shakespearean sonnet has four parts—three **quatrains** and a **couplet** at the end. Its rhyme scheme is *abab cdcd efef gg.*

speaker the voice that speaks in a poem. The speaker may or may not be the poet. Often the poet assumes a **persona,** or alternate identity. *See* **narrator.**

stanza a group of lines in a poem. Each stanza in a rhyming poem often has the same **rhyme scheme.** *See* **quatrain.**

stress the emphasis given to a word or syllable. A strongly stressed syllable is marked with a straight line (/) and an unstressed syllable is marked with a curved line (∪), as in this example:

/ ∪ / ∪ /∪ /
Twinkle, twinkle, little star

structure the overall design of a work. Structure refers to the way a poet arranges words, lines, and ideas to produce a particular effect.

symbol a person, place, or thing that stands for something else.

tercet three lines that may or may not contain end rhyme.

theme the insight or message that an author conveys in a piece of writing.

third-person point of view the point of view, or perspective, in which the speaker stands outside the action and tells the story using words such as *he*, *she*, and *they*. *See* **first-person point of view** and **point of view.**

tone a writer's attitude toward his or her subject, audience, or self.

trochee a metrical **foot** consisting of one stressed and one unstressed syllable in which the stressed syllable regularly comes first (/ ∪).

verse paragraph a group of lines in a poem that forms a unit similar to that of a prose paragraph. A verse paragraph's length varies according to the requirements of the thought that is being expressed.

villanelle a nineteen-line poem composed of five **tercets** and an ending **quatrain**. The first and third lines of the first tercet are repeated alternately as the third line of the other tercets and as the third and fourth lines of the quatrain. The best-known villanelle is "Do Not Go Gentle into That Good Night" by Dylan Thomas.

continued from page iv

Sandburg, Carl. "Cool Tombs" from *Cornhuskers* by Carl Sandburg. Copyright 1918 by Holt, Rinehart and Winston and renewed 1946 by Carl Sandburg. Reprinted by permission of Harcourt Brace & Company.

Sandburg, Carl. "Flying Fish" from *Smoke and Steel* by Carl Sandburg. Copyright 1920 by Harcourt Brace & Company and renewed 1948 by Carl Sandburg. Reprinted by permission of the publisher.

Sexton, Anne. "Cinderella" from *Transformations*. Copyright © 1971 by Anne Sexton. Reprinted by permission of Houghton Mifflin Co. All rights reserved.

Spinden, Herbert J. "Song of the Sky Loom" from *Songs of the Tewa*, translated by Herbert J. Spinden. Reprinted by permission of Sunstone Press, NM.

Spivack, Kathleen. "March 1st" from *Flying Inland* by Kathleen Spivack. Copyright © 1965, 1966, 1967, 1968, 1970, 1971, 1973 by Kathleen Spivack. Used by permission of Doubleday, a division of Bantam Doubleday Dell Publishing Group, Inc.

Starbird, Kaye. "Idaho" from *A Snail's A Failure Socially and Other Poems, Mostly About People* by Kaye Starbird. Copyright © 1966 by Kaye Starbird. Copyright renewed 1994 by Catharine D. Slawson. Reprinted by permission of Marian Reiner.

Stone, Ruth. "In an Iridescent Time" from *Second-Hand Coat* by Ruth Stone, 1987. Reprinted by permission of the author.

Strand, Mark. "Keeping Things Whole" from *Selected Poems* by Mark Strand. Copyright © 1979, 1980 by Mark Strand. Reprinted by permission of Alfred A. Knopf, Inc.

Tapahonso, Luci. "I Am Singing Now" from *A Breeze Swept Through* by Luci Tapahonso. Copyright © 1987 by Luci Tapahonso. Reprinted by permission of the author.

Teasdale, Sara. "Solitary" is reprinted with the permission of Simon & Schuster from *The Collected Poems of Sara Teasdale*. Copyright © 1926 by Macmillan Publishing Company, renewed 1954 by Mamie T. Wheless.

Wright, Richard. "The spring lingers on" and "The crow flew so fast" by Richard Wright. Copyright © 1959 by Richard Wright. Published by Arcade Publishing, Inc. New York, NY. Reprinted by permission.